TOP **10**
PRAGUE

CONTENTS

PRAGUE

INTRODUCING

Charles Bridge illuminated at sunset

WELCOME TO
PRAGUE

Prague has firmly established itself as one of Europe's most popular cities, where Art Nouveau masterpieces line medieval streets and the planet's best beer is enjoyed on Baroque squares. Don't want to miss a thing? With Top 10 Prague, you'll enjoy the very best the city has to offer.

The City of a Hundred Spires, Prague has a way of enchanting everyone who strolls its cobbled lanes. It's been fortunate enough over the centuries to have escaped both extensive war damage and the makeovers of over-zealous urban planners. The result? A central core that has changed little since the 14th century, when Prague was the capital of the Holy Roman Empire. A stroll past the Gothic and Baroque buildings on the Old Town Square is to wind back the centuries, the Old Town Hall's Astronomical Clock still chiming by the hour as you follow the coronation route of the

Overlooking the Vltava river

Bohemian kings over Charles Bridge up to Prague Castle. Pretty buildings are Prague's DNA; you never have to walk too far to stumble upon epic cathedrals like St Vitus or fairytale churches like Loreta. And the city's rich history doesn't stop there, with the snaggletooth headstones of the Old Jewish Cemetery testifying to the city's once thriving Jewish community.

Prague is a historic city through and through, but to focus too much on the past is to overlook all that the city offers today. For starters, there's the world-class beer scene, where a dewy half-litre of golden Czech lager or a mug of Pilsner Urquell might well be the best – and some of the cheapest – beer in the world. Then there's the art scene, with David Černý's darkly humorous public art making the city an open-air gallery, and the epic National Gallery showcasing modern pieces across multiple locations. Better still, Prague has enough green spaces to make you forget all about bridges and castles, from the lush slopes of Petřín Hill to former monastery orchards.

So, where to start? With Top 10 Prague, of course. This pocket-sized guide gets to the heart of the city with simple lists of ten, expert local knowledge and comprehensive maps, helping you turn an ordinary trip into an extraordinary one.

THE STORY OF
PRAGUE

Prague's story is a turbulent tale. What began as a castle on a rocky outcrop would rise to become the seat of an empire before declining into a backwater of the Habsburg Empire. In the 20th century alone it assumed numerous identities before eventually becoming the capital of the Czech Republic. And yet, despite the setbacks, the city has risen again, stronger after each fall. Here's the story of how it came to be.

Prague Begins

Evidence of human activity here dates back to the Paleolithic era, but it wasn't until the 4th century BCE that Celtic tribes built settlements around modern-day Prague. Germanic tribes followed in the 1st century BCE with the first Slavs arriving in the 6th century CE. These new arrivals clashed with the existing tribes and their struggles led to the emergence of the first ruling Slavic dynasty of the Bohemian region, the Přemyslid dynasty, in around 800. They consolidated their position by constructing fortified settlements at Vyšehrad and where Prague Castle stands today; these buildings marked the foundation of Prague. Thanks to the security offered by these fortifications, the settlements grew and prospered, and in 950, the Bohemian Kingdom was subsumed into the Holy Roman Empire.

A City Emerges

Despite being one of the most powerful regions within the German-dominated Holy Roman Empire, the nascent city of Prague was still a collection of separate settlements. Only in 1172 was the first stone bridge, Judith Bridge, built across the Vltava, joining the existing villages. In the century that followed Staré Město (Old Town) and Malá Strana (the Little Quarter) were established, the latter as an area for German migrants to settle in. It was also at this time that Prague's Jews began to be confined to what would become the Jewish Ghetto.

Seat of Empire

The Přemyslid dynasty, which ruled Prague for nearly five centuries, came to an end in 1306 with the murder of its ruler. Power was transferred to John of Luxembourg, kickstarting a golden era

Radical Czech theologian and philosopher, Jan Hus

that continued under his son Charles IV, who would also become Holy Roman Emperor. Charles made Prague the capital of his empire and successfully transformed it into a leading European city; he founded a university, commissioned Charles Bridge, laid out Nové Město (New Town) and commenced the construction of St Vitus Cathedral.

Religious Strife

But with highs came lows. In 1389 anti-Jewish pogroms saw around 3,000 of Prague's Jews murdered. Not long after, in 1415, the radical Prague Hussite preacher Jan Hus was burned at the stake in Germany after railing against immoral practices of the church. His death instigated the Hussite wars – two decades of fighting between Protestants and Catholics that resulted in Catholic victory. In 1526, the Catholic Habsburgs became rulers of Prague and began to crush Protestantism. Their efforts led to the second defenestration in 1618, when a group of Protestant noblemen threw three Catholic officials from a window of Prague Castle. This helped spark the Thirty Years' War and the Protestant defeat in 1620 at the Battle of White Mountain, west of Prague. The result for Prague was Habsburg rule for the next 300 years and relegation from imperial capital to provincial city.

Charles IV and the foundation stone of the Charles Bridge

Moments in History

9th century
The founding of Prague, with the first sites constructed on Vyšehrad hill.

1348
Bohemian king Charles IV becomes Holy Roman Emperor and makes Prague his capitcal.

1415
Radical Bohemian preacher Jan Hus is burned at the stake, leading to decades of religious war.

1618
The Defenestration at Prague Castle plays a key role in inciting the Thirty Years' War, which decimates Prague.

1620
The Habsburgs win the Battle of the White Mountain, near to today's airport, ending Prague's prominence within the Holy Roman Empire.

1918
The Independent Czechoslovakia Republic is founded at the end of World War I with Tomáš Masaryk elected as its first president.

1939–1945
Nazis invade and occupy Prague during World War II.

1948
The Czechoslovak Communist Party takes power in a coup.

1968
The liberal reforms of the Prague Spring are brutally crushed by a Soviet Union-led invasion.

1989
The student-led "Velvet Revolution" contributes to the downfall of the Communist government.

2022–present
Czechs welcome hundreds of thousands of Ukrainian refugees fleeing the war with Russia.

National Revival

Things would get worse before they got better. The rest of the 17th century saw plague and a great fire in 1689. The Habsburgs used this as an opportunity to rebuild the city in Baroque style. Great new buildings, gardens and churches, including the National Theatre and Clementinum, were built in this period. The city became a hub of industrialization with a population that doubled in the 18th century and would continue to grow. In 1784, the four towns of Prague (Staré Město, Nové Město, Malá Strana and Hradčany) were merged into a single, unified city. As Prague expanded so did the collective idea of a "Czech" identity among all strata of society. The populace briefly revolted in 1848, and though this was quickly and brutally suppressed, the ruling Habsburgs began to loosen their grip in the decades that followed, thus allowing the Czech people to rediscover their history and culture.

Czechoslovakia and World War II

Following the collapse of the Austro-Hungarian Empire in 1918, an independent Czech and Slovak state (Czechoslovakia) was founded, with Prague as its capital. The new country initially prospered both economically and culturally under the leadership of President Tomáš Masaryk, but the Great Depression and then the rise of Adolf

Nazi leader Adolf Hitler meets a group of German students in Prague

President Petr Pavel with German President Frank-Walter Steinmeier

Hitler halted such growth. Just 20 years after its foundation, Czechoslovakia was surrendered to Nazi Germany as part of the Munich Agreement. In March 1939 Prague was occupied by the Nazis. The city suffered heavily during World War II, both from Nazi persecution of its citizens, especially the Jewish population (which has never recovered), and a number of Allied bombing raids. In May 1945, Prague was liberated following a citywide uprising and the arrival of the Soviet Red Army.

Communism and Freedom

In the first free election following the war, in 1946, the Czechoslovak Communist Party won a plurality of support from a war-weary population. Perhaps emboldened by this, the Communists consolidated power in a coup and Prague remained under the Soviet sphere of influence for the next four decades. The early years saw brutal repression as a Soviet-style dictatorship was imposed, but by the 1960s there was hope for change. This came to fruition in 1968, when Communist leader Alexander Dubček introduced a series of liberal reforms known as the "Prague Spring". The movement was ruthlessly crushed by a massive Soviet-led military invasion on 21 August 1968. The harsh rule that followed became known as the period of "normalization" by Czechs and gave rise to an underground dissident movement of writers, actors and intellectuals who later spearheaded the 1989 "Velvet Revolution". After weeks of nationwide protests, the Communists fell to public pressure and playwright Václav Havel became president.

Prague Today

The early years of the post-Communist transition were marked by huge political and economic shifts towards capitalism, and the peaceful split of Czechoslovakia into two states on 1 January 1993. The Czech Republic gradually integrated into Europe, joining NATO in 1999 and the European Union in 2004. Prague has also become one of Europe's biggest tourist destinations and one of its most celebrated historic cities, thanks to the preservation of its stunning medieval architecture. The past decade has seen the country become increasingly divided over immigration and face key issues related to high inflation and climate change. In December 2023 the city was shocked by a mass shooting that left 14 dead and many injured. Yet Prague has tackled these challenges head on, toughening its gun laws and introducing climate solutions. Most importantly, it remains an open city as evidenced by the roughly 500,000 Ukrainian refugees Prague has welcomed since 2022.

TOP 10
EXPERIENCES

Planning the perfect trip to Prague? Whether you're visiting for the first time or making a return trip, there are some things you simply shouldn't miss out on. To make the most of your time, and to enjoy the best this popular Central European capital has to offer, be sure to add these experiences to your list.

1 See architectural marvels
Where staggeringly beautiful buildings are concerned, Prague has an embarrassment of riches. Majestic architecture awaits on every corner, whether it's the Old Town Hall *(p30)* with its Astronomical Clock, the magnificent St Nicholas Church *(p98)* or the Baroque masterpiece that is Prague Castle *(p22)*.

2 Enjoy highbrow culture evenings
Classical music is the lifeblood of Prague and the opera and theatre scenes are world-class (and yet, reasonably priced). Check out the esteemed shows at the National Theatre *(p120)* or see concerts at the Rudolfinum *(p73)* or Smetana Hall at the Municipal House *(p89)*.

3 Drink great beer
Lift a glass of Czech beer and you'll understand why Czechs drink more of the stuff per capita than any nation on earth: the beer here is simply excellent. Join the locals for a pint of beloved local lager, Pilsner Urquell, or seek out tipples such as Únětice, Budvar and Prague's own Staropramen.

4 Take in the view
Prague's historic core is blessed with a crown of surrounding hills that offer breathtaking vistas over the city's shapely spires, cupolas and bridges. Snap a classic skyline photo from the hilltops of Letná Park *(p128)*, Strahov Monastery or Petřín Hill *(p46)*; they're all equally iconic.

5 Eat like a royal

Hearty and delicious, Czech food is about flavours and textures. Ensure you try local favourites goulash (a paprika-enriched stew) and *svíčková* (roast beef in a sauce). Then there's the national dish: roast pork, best served with soft dumplings to soak up that rich gravy.

6 Relax in parks and gardens

Tucked away behind ornate walls or flanking Renaissance palaces, Prague's historic gardens are tranquil oases. Don't miss the Baroque Palace Gardens (p67), the Renaissance Wallenstein Garden (p83) or the lovely Vrtba Garden (p99), which stretches over three ornate levels.

7 Catch an ice-hockey match

Many locals live for the frenetic thrill of ice-hockey, the Czech national sport. See the best players in action at the O2 Arena, where visiting teams battle with hometown HC Sparta Praha. The excitement on the ice is matched by the feverish enthusiasm in the stands.

8 Chill with coffee and cake

Move over Paris and Vienna: Prague's coffee culture can match any city in Europe. Relax over a perfect cappuccino in Café Slavia (p94) or sip a quick espresso in Café Louvre (p124). Pair your coffee with an apple strudel, pancakes or honey-cake (*medovník*).

9 Admire unusual art

It might be home to masterpieces of European art, but Prague also celebrates its weird side. Local shock-artist David Černý's hanging horse (p68) and rotating Kafka head are worth a visit, while the mysterious headless statue by Jaroslav Róna is a transfixing oddity.

10 Discover Communist History

Simply walking through Prague, passing sites such as the memorial at Petřín Hill and Žižkov TV Tower (p128), offers a primer in Communist history. For a lesson on the years of dictatorship, visit the Museum of Communism (p122).

ITINERARIES

Seeing the Old Town Square, enjoying beer in a local pub or beer hall, visiting the ancient Prague Castle: there's a lot to see and do in Prague. With places to eat, drink or take in the view, these itineraries offer ways to spend 2 days and 4 days in the capital.

2 DAYS

Day 1

Morning

Start your exploration of Prague at the striking Art Nouveau Municipal House (*Obecní dům, p89*) and the medieval Powder Gate (*p89*), where Bohemian kings once began their coronation route to Prague Castle. Follow in their foot-steps through the gate, heading down Celetná street with its many shops and cafés until you reach the Old Town Square (*p28*). Stand at its centre to appreciate the varied architecture of the Old Town Hall, the Church of Our Lady before Týn and the Astronomical Clock – where you can see the clock's procession of the 12 Apostles.

Afternoon

Wander over to the Vltava river and ascend the steps of the astronomical tower of the Clementinum (*p90*), a former Jesuit college, for stunning views

 DRINK
You're never far from a pub in the centre of town. Good options – for both a beer and a meal – include U Fleků (*p124*) and Pivovar Národní (*pivovarnarodni.cz*).

over Charles Bridge (*p32*) before a pitstop for a hearty lunch and a Pilsner at V Zátiší (*p95*). Then it's time to stroll over to the two sites of the National Museum (*p44*) at the top of the vast Wenceslas Square (*p42*). A whole afternoon can be spent exploring the history, science and kids exhibits in both the beautiful main building and the annex, which are conveniently linked by a tunnel. Finish your first day with tasty Czech dishes at Restaurace Bredovský dvůr (*p125*).

Historic streets in the centre of Prague's Old Town

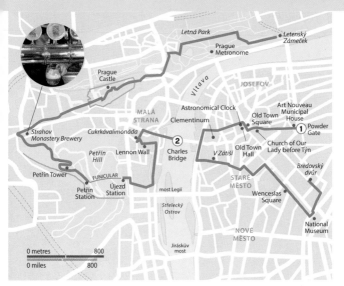

Day 2

Morning
Your second day is all about the other side of the river. Get up early to cross the iconic Charles Bridge (p32) before the crowds build up. Having crossed, grab coffee at Cukrkávalimonáda (p102) and meander through the quiet streets of Mála Strana – Beatles fans should pay a visit to the graffiti-clad Lennon Wall (p82). Leave the city streets behind and take the funicular up to the greenery of Petřín Hill (p46), one of Prague's largest parks, home to woodlands, beautiful gardens and a hilariously unflattering mirror maze. Be sure to take in the dramatic views down to Staré Město.

Afternoon
Enjoy a languorous lunch at the Strahov Monastery Brewery (p108)

VIEW
Don't pay to climb Petřín Tower – the view is just as good from the trails heading north from the tower towards Prague Castle and Strahov Monastery.

before tackling St Vitus Cathedral and the labyrinth of historic sights that comprises Prague Castle (p22), such as St George's Basilica, Lobkowicz Palace and Golden Lane. Spend as much time as you need soaking in the history here before heading to your final stop, Letná Park (p128). Once in Letná, make a bee-line for the towering metronome (p52) – the largest functioning metronome in the world – and Letenský zámeček restaurant (letenskyzamecek.cz) in the park's eastern end. This is the perfect spot to enjoy a meal and a well-earned drink in the beer garden as the sun sets.

Beer garden with a view at Letenský zámeček

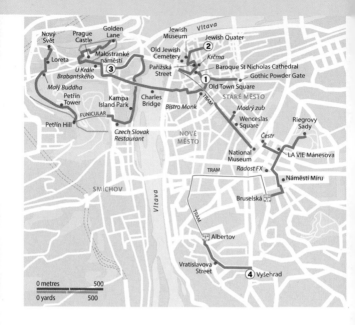

4 DAYS

Day 1

There are few better places to start a trip through Prague than Staré Město. Begin with a tour of the city's architecture in the streets around Old Town Square (p28). Look out for the variety of styles on show: the medieval Gothic Powder Gate (p89), the Art Nouveau Municipal House (p89), and the Baroque St Nicholas Cathedral (p90). Soak up the lively atmosphere in the square itself with a lunch of fresh produce at Bistro Monk (p95). before you head over to Prague Castle (p22) for the afternoon, crossing the iconic Charles Bridge (p32) on the way. Learn about the castle's

Medieval Astronomical clock on the Old Town Hall

fascinating history at the Prague Castle Story exhibition and then pop into the castle's other sites – Golden Lane is worth seeing. End your sojourn through history with dinner at the medieval-styled U Krále Brabantského (p109).

Day 2

Devote your morning to the historic Jewish Quarter, Josefov, beginning with

> **EAT**
> Don't overlook the restaurants around Old Town Square. Amid the touristy spots are hidden gems like 420 (420restaurant.cz), helmed by Michelin-starred Radek Kašpárek.

> ☕ **DRINK**
> Eschew the big name beers for the Vinohradský Pivovar micro-brewer in Vinohrady *(vinohradsky pivovar.cz)*. Pair one of the beers with the brewery's tasty Czech food.

the seven sites of the Jewish Museum *(p36)*. Learn about Jewish culture and history and don't miss the fascinating Old Jewish Cemetery *(p113)*. Give yourself a break between each site with some retail therapy in the bespoke shops on Pařížská street, and then enjoy a lunch of classic Bohemian dishes at Krčma *(p117)*. Jump on tram A at Staroměstská Můstek to leap forward in time with a visit to Wenceslas Square *(p42)*, in Nové Město. Soak in the Art Nouveau palaces found around the square and then its off to the top of the square for a couple of hours in the National Museum *(p44)*, home to exhibits on everything from minerals to communism. Before you leave, admire the incredible frescoes found in the entrance hall. End the day with fine Thai fare at Modrý zub *(p125)* and a drink at one of the many excellent bars that surround Wenceslas Square.

Day 3

Today it's time to see the greener side of Prague. Start in the sprawling Malostranské Náměstí square, with its beautiful palace arcades and fabulous Baroque St Nicholas Church *(p98)*. From here, you can enjoy a leisurely amble through Kampa Island park *(p98)* right on the Vltava river – look out for the oddly transfixing sculptures of faceless babies in the park – with a stop at the somewhat unimaginatively named Czech Slovak Restaurant *(p103)* for a lunch of modern Czech cuisine. Refuelled, catch the funicular to the top of Petřín Hill *(p46)* where you can enjoy an afternoon in this grand forested park. Just make sure you climb the 299 steps of Petřín Tower – a copy of the Eiffel Tower – for unsurpassed views over Prague. Afterwards, find the trail that

leads north to Loreta *(p34)* where you can dine on superb east Asian cuisine at the vegan Malý Buddha *(p109)*, before a stroll along tranquil Nový Svět *(p106)*.

Day 4

Your final day is all about Prague's less-visited spots. Hop on metro line C to lofty Vyšehrad *(p127)*, a fort believed to be the ancient seat of Czech princes. Explore the rotunda and cemetery, where over 600 famous Czechs are buried, before walking down sloping Vratislavova street to admire Cubist houses. Hop on tram 5 from Albertov to Bruselská and then wander over to LA VIE Mánesova for a leisurely lunch *(tekutemaso.cz)*. The afternoon can then be spent exploring the shops of leafy Náměstí Míru and attractive Vinohrady. As the sun begins to dip, walk over to Riegrovy Sady park; if you're lucky, there'll be a beautiful sunset over the valley. Dine at the Čestr *(p125)* meat smokehouse and then party your last night away at Radost FX *(p123)*.

Centuries-old stairs leading down to Novy Svet

TOP 10 HIGHLIGHTS

Old Town Square

EXPLORE THE
HIGHLIGHTS

There are some sights in Prague you simply shouldn't miss, and it's these attractions that make the Top 10. Discover what makes each one a must-see on the following pages.

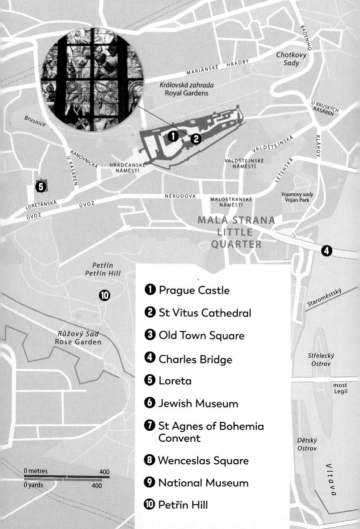

NA ZÁTORCE

MARIÁNSKÉ HRADBY

BADENIHO

Chotkovy Sady

Královská zahrada
Royal Gardens

U BRUSKÝCH KASÁREN

Brusnice

KANOVNICKÁ

U KASÁREN

HRADČANSKÉ NÁMĚSTÍ

VALDŠTEJNSKÁ

VALDŠTEJNSKÉ NÁMĚSTÍ

LETENSKÁ

KLÁROV

LORETÁNSKÁ

ÚVOZ

ÚVOZ

NERUDOVA

MALOSTRANSKÉ NÁMĚSTÍ

Vojanovy sady
Vojan Park

MALÁ STRANA
LITTLE
QUARTER

Petřín
Petřín Hill

Staroměstský

Růžový Sad
Rose Garden

Střelecký Ostrov

most Legií

Dětský Ostrov

Vltava

❶ Prague Castle

❷ St Vitus Cathedral

❸ Old Town Square

❹ Charles Bridge

❺ Loreta

❻ Jewish Museum

❼ St Agnes of Bohemia Convent

❽ Wenceslas Square

❾ National Museum

❿ Petřín Hill

0 metres 400
0 yards 400

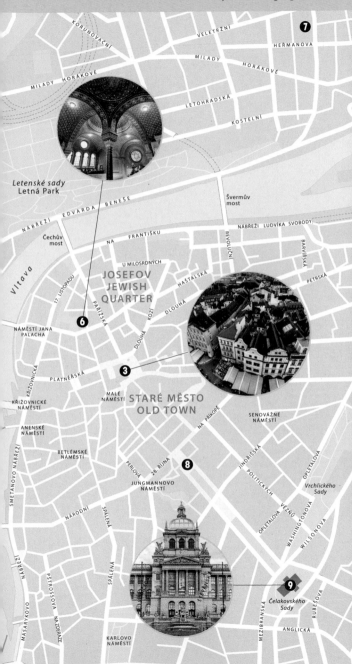

KORUNOVAČNÍ

VELETRŽNÍ

HEŘMANOVA

MILADY

HORÁKOVÉ

MILADY HORÁKOVÉ

LETOHRADSKÁ

KOŠTELNÍ

Letenské sady
Letná Park

EDVARDA BENEŠE

Švermův
most

NÁBŘEŽÍ

NÁBŘEŽÍ LUDVÍKA SVOBODY

Čechův
most

NA FRANTIŠKU

REVOLUČNÍ

BARVÍŘSKÁ

Vltava

U MILOSRDNÝCH

**JOSEFOV
JEWISH
QUARTER**

HAŠTALSKÁ

PETRSKÁ

17. LISTOPADU

PAŘÍŽSKÁ

KOZÍ

DLOUHÁ

DLOUHÁ

NÁMĚSTÍ JANA
PALACHA

KŘIŽOVNICKÁ

PLATNÉŘSKÁ

KŘIŽOVNICKÉ
NÁMĚSTÍ

MALÉ
NÁMĚSTÍ

**STARÉ MĚSTO
OLD TOWN**

ANENSKÉ
NÁMĚSTÍ

NA PŘÍKOPĚ

SENOVÁŽNÉ
NÁMĚSTÍ

SMETANOVO NÁBŘEŽÍ

BETLÉMSKÉ
NÁMĚSTÍ

PERLOVÁ

28. ŘÍJNA

JINDŘIŠSKÁ

VRCHLICKÉHO

OPLETALOVA

JUNGMANNOVO
NÁMĚSTÍ

POLITICKÝCH

*Vrchlického
Sady*

NÁRODNÍ

SPÁLENÁ

OPLETALOVA

VĚZŇŮ

WASHINGTONOVA

WILSONOVA

NÁBŘEŽÍ

SPÁLENÁ

ŠTĚPÁNSKÁ

MASARYKOVO

PŠTROSSOVA

NA ZDERAZE

MEZIBRÁNSKÁ

*Čelakovského
Sady*

RUBEŠOVA

KARLOVO
NÁMĚSTÍ

ANGLICKÁ

PRAGUE CASTLE

C2 **Hradčany** **9am–5pm daily** **hrad.cz**

Prague Castle (*Pražský hrad*) is the metaphorical and historical throne of the Czech lands. Around 880 CE, Prince Bořivoj built a wooden fortress on this hilltop, establishing it as the dynastic base of the Přemyslids. In the 14th century the castle became the seat of the Holy Roman Empire. Much of it was rebuilt by Empress Maria Theresa in the 18th century. Today the castle is the official residence of the Czech president.

1 Old Royal Palace

While Prince Bořivoj made do with a wooden structure, subsequent residences were built on top of each other as the tastes of Bohemia's rulers changed (*p25*).

2 South Gardens

Emperor Ferdinand I gave the castle some greenery in the late 16th century, and First Republic architect Josip Plečnik created the lined paths, steps and grottoes.

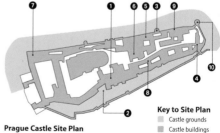

Prague Castle Site Plan

Key to Site Plan
- Castle grounds
- Castle buildings

3 White Tower

The castle's White Tower was once used as a prison. Today, shops here sell grisly souvenirs. The gangways from which archers once watched over the moat are lined with replicas of weapons.

4 Lobkowicz Palace

The only privately owned building in the castle complex, this rival to the National Gallery holds works by Bruegel, Canaletto, Dürer, Rubens and Velázquez.

5 St George's Convent

Prince Boleslav II, with Princess Mlada,

Prague Castle looming over the Vltava

still admire the statues of St Peter and St Paul on the façade.

8 Rosenberg Palace

This 16th-century palace has had multiple uses: as an 18th-century residence for noble-women, as part of the Ministry of Internal Affairs of Czechoslovakia, and as modern presidential offices.

established the first Czech convent for Benedictine nuns here in 973 CE.

6 St George's Basilica

Prince Vratislav built the basilica around 920 CE. The 13th-century chapel of St Ludmila is decorated with beautiful 16th-century paintings.

7 Chapel of the Holy Cross

Built by the Italian architect Anselmo Lurago in 1763, this chapel is usually closed, but you can

9 Golden Lane

In order to avoid paying guild dues in town, goldsmiths lived in these colourful little houses.

10 Daliborka Tower

When captured, Dalibor, a Czech Robin Hood figure, became the first prisoner of the tower that now bears his name.

Clockwise from right
The ceiling fresco in St George's Basilica; coats of arms on the walls of the Old Royal Palace; colourful houses lining Golden Lane

CASTLE GUIDE
Most of the grounds are free to enter, but tickets to see the interiors are sold at the information centres in the second and third courtyards. Standard tickets include entry to the Old Royal Palace, St George's Basilica, St Vitus Cathedral and Golden Lane (including Daliborka Tower). You can add on the Great South Tower and The Story of Prague Castle *(p25)* exhibition for extra fees.

Old Royal Palace Features

Intricate rib vaulting at Vladislav Hall

1. Vladislav Hall
Here, Benedikt Rejt created a mastery of Gothic design with the elaborate vaulting. It has been used for coronations and jousting tournaments, and, since the First Republic, the country's presidents have been ceremoniously sworn in here.

2. Louis Wing
Only ten years and a few steps separate the southern wing from the main hall, but in that brief space, Rejt moved castle architecture from Gothic to Renaissance. Bohemian nobles met here in an administrative body when the king was away.

3. Bohemian Chancellery
Protestant noblemen threw two Catholic governors and their secretary from the east window, sparking the Thirty Years' War. Their fall was broken by a dung heap – or an intervening angel, depending on who you ask.

4. Old Land Rolls Room
The coats of arms on the walls belong to clerks who tracked property ownership and court decisions from 1614 to 1777. Until Maria Theresa, records were unnumbered, identified only by elaborate covers.

5. Riders' Staircase
The low steps and vaulted ceiling of this stairway permitted mounted knights to make grand entrances to the spectacular jousting tournaments held in Vladislav Hall.

6. Chapel of All Saints
A door leads from Vladislav Hall to a balcony above the Chapel of All Saints, modelled by Petr Parléř on Paris's Gothic Sainte-Chapelle. After fire destroyed it in 1541, it was redesigned in Renaissance style. Of particular artistic note is Hans van Aachen's *Triptych of the Angels*.

7. Soběslav Residence
Prince Soběslav built the first stone palace in the 12th century.

8. The Story of Prague Castle
This informative and entertaining exhibition covers the history, events, personalities, and arts and crafts relating to the main castle complex.

9. Busts from Petr Parléř's Workshop
These impressive effigies, created in the late 14th century, include the grandfather-father-grandson set of John of Luxembourg, Charles IV and Wenceslas IV.

10. Diet
Bohemian nobles met the king here in a prototype parliament. The king sat on the throne (the one seen today is a 19th-century replica), the archbishop sat on his right, while the estates sat on his left. The portraits on the wall show, from the left, Maria Theresa, her husband Franz, Josef II, Leopold II and Franz I, who fought Napoleon at Austerlitz.

PRAGUE'S DEFENESTRATIONS

Prague's first recorded instance of execution by hurling the condemned people from a window occurred at the outset of the Hussite Wars in 1419. Vladislav II's officials met a similar fate in 1483. Perhaps as a tribute to their forebears, more than 100 Protestant nobles stormed the Old Royal Palace in 1618 and cast two hated Catholic governors and their secretary out of the window. Protestants said the men's fall was broken by a dung heap swept from the Vladislav Hall after a recent tournament, while Catholics claimed they were saved by angels. The incident is often cited as the spark that began the Thirty Years' War. After the defeat of the Protestants by the army of the Holy Roman Emperor Ferdinand II at the first skirmish at White Mountain *(p30)*, 27 of these nobles were executed in the Old Town Square *(p28)*.

Clash between Protestant and Catholic forces at White Mountain

ST VITUS CATHEDRAL

📍 C2 🏛 Third Courtyard, Prague Castle 🕐 Apr–Oct: 9am–5pm Mon–Sat, noon–5pm Sun; Nov–Mar: 9am–4pm daily 🌐 hatedralasvatehovita.cz ♿

The spectacular Gothic *Katedrála svatého Víta* is an unmissable sight in Prague, not least because of its dominant position on Hradčany hill. Prince Wenceslas first built a rotunda here on a pagan worship site and dedicated it to St Vitus (*svatý Vít*), a Roman saint.

The soaring Great South Tower

is clear. When work resumed after the war, architectural preferences had moved towards the Renaissance, hence the rounded cap that can be seen on a Gothic base.

1 Great South Tower

The point at which the Hussite Wars halted construction of this 96-m (315-ft) tower

2 Royal Crypt

The greatest kings of Bohemia are buried in a single room beneath the cathedral, including Charles IV, Wenceslas IV and Rudolf II.

3 High Altar

Bounded by St Vitus Chapel and the marble sarcophagi of Ferdinand I and

TOP TIP

The Royal Crypt can only be accessed through a guided tour.

family, the high altar and chancel follow Neo-Gothic philosophy.

4 Golden Portal

This triple-arched arcade was the main cathedral entrance until the western end was completed in the 20th century. It is still used on special occasions.

St Wenceslas's tomb, Wenceslas Chapel

5 Bohemian Crown Jewels

You'd think there would be a safer place for the crown and sceptre of Bohemia, but the coronation chamber of Wenceslas Chapel is said to be guarded by the spirit of the saint.

6 The Tomb of St John of Nepomuk

The silver for this 1,680-kg (3,700-lb) coffin came from the Bohemian mining town Kutná Hora, signified by the miners' statues to the left of the tomb.

7 New Archbishop's Chapel

Czech artists Alfons Mucha created the Art Nouveau window

Neo-Gothic interior of the cathedral

of the Slavic saints for the chapel. Despite appearances, the glass is painted, not stained.

8 Sigismund

One of four Renaissance bells in the Great South Tower, the 18-tonne bell (20 ton) known as Sigismund is the nation's largest and dates from 1549. It takes four volunteers to ring the bell on important church holidays and at events.

9 Royal Oratory

The royals crossed a narrow bridge from the Old Royal Palace (p22) to this private gallery for Mass. The coats of arms represent all the countries ruled by Vladislav II.

10 Wenceslas Chapel

This stands on the site of the first rotunda and

contains St Wenceslas's tomb. The frescoes of Christ's Passion on the lower wall are surrounded by 1,300 semi-precious stones. To celebrate his son Ludvik's coronation, Vladislav II commissioned the upper frescoes of St Wenceslas's life.

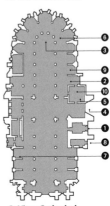

St Vitus Cathedral Floorplan

OLD TOWN SQUARE

📍 M3 🏛 Staré Město

As the heart and soul of the city, the Old Town Square (*Staroměstské náměstí*) is hard to miss. There was a marketplace here in the 11th century, but it was in 1338, when John of Luxembourg gave Prague's burghers permission to form a town council, that the Old Town Hall was built and the square came into its own. Today, it has a lively atmosphere, with café tables set out in front of painted façades.

1 Dům u Minuty
The "House at the Minute" probably takes its name from the not-so-minute *sgraffito* images on its walls. The alchemical symbols adorning Staroměstské náměstí 2 date from 1610. Writer Franz Kafka (*p56*) lived in the black-and-white house as a boy, from 1889 to 1896.

2 House at the Stone Bell
Formerly done up in Baroque style, workers discovered the Gothic façade of this house as late as 1980. On the southwestern corner is the bell which gives the house its name. The Municipal Gallery often hosts temporary exhibitions here.

3 Church of Our Lady before Týn
This Gothic edifice began as a humble church (*p51*) serving residents in the

Stunning *sgraffito* on Dům u Minuty

**Prague's famous
Old Town Square**

5 Jan Hus Memorial

Hus was burned at the stake in 1415 for proposing radical church reform. The inscription below his figure at the 1915 memorial reads "Truth Will Prevail".

6 Marian Column

On Czechoslovakia's declaration of independence in 1918, this former column reminded jubilant mobs of Habsburg rule and they tore it down. In 2020, the column was reconstructed.

7 Ungelt

The courtyard behind Týn church was home to foreign merchants in the 14th century, but today it houses smart boutiques and cafés.

8 Kinský Palace

This Rococo palace, found at Staroměstské náměstí 12, now houses the National Gallery's temporary exhibitions (p122). It was once home to the haberdashery owned by Franz Kafka's father, Hermann.

9 Malé náměstí

The ornate well in the centre of the "Small Square" doubles as a plague memorial. The elaborate murals of crafters on the façade of Rott House were designed by Mikoláš Aleš. From the 19th century to the early 1990s, the building was an ironmongery.

10 Štorch House

At Staroměstské náměstí 16, the focal points are Art Nouveau paintings of St Wenceslas (the patron saint of Bohemia) and the three Magi.

JAN HUS

The rector of Prague University, Jan Hus was dedicated to fighting against corruption in the church. Declared a heretic by the church, he was burned at the stake. Czech resentment turned into civil war, with Hussite rebels facing the power of Rome. But the Hussites split into moderate and radical factions. Hus is still a national figure – 6 July, the day he was killed, is a public holiday.

EAT
Take a break from the sites at the historic Restaurace Mincovna found in the corner of the square (restaurace mincovna.cz).

---

mercantile town (týn) in the 14th century. Following architectural customs of the time, the south tower is stouter than the north one; they are said to depict Adam and Eve.

4 St Nicholas Cathedral

Prague has two Baroque churches of St Nicholas, both built by Kilian Ignac Dientzenhofer. The architect completed the one, called the cathedral now, in Staré Město two years before starting Malá Strana's (p96). Regular concerts here are worth a visit.

Jan Hus Memorial in Old Town Square

Old Town Hall Features

1. Astronomical Clock
During the day, bells ring, cocks crow and 15th-century statues dance on the hour while crowds of tourists watch from below.

2. Apostles
Marionette artist Vojtěch Sucharda carved the 12 wooden figures that emerge from the clock every hour – they replace the ones destroyed by German artillery in 1945.

3. Municipal Hall
This was once the central point of the building where all the most important matters concerning the administration of Prague's Staré Město were discussed.

4. Dukla Memorial
Behind a brass plaque marked with the year 1944 is a pot of soil from the Dukla battlefield. German artillery killed and wounded around 70,000 Red Army soldiers in this Slovak pass in one of the most grievous Soviet miscalculations of World War II.

5. White Mountain Memorial
In the pavement on the town hall's eastern side are set 27 crosses in memory of the Bohemian nobles who were executed for their role in the Thirty Years' War. After the Battle of White Mountain *(p9)*, the men were publicly hanged, beheaded or drawn and quartered here.

6. Gothic Chapel
The small chapel adjoining the Mayors' Hall was consecrated in 1381 in honour of Sts Wenceslas, Vitus and Ludmila. Wenceslas IV's emblem and his wife Eufemia's initial adorn the entrance portal. In the nave is a model of the Marian column *(p29)* which stood on the square until 1918 and was returned in 2020.

Spiral staircase leading to the Astronomical Clock

7. Elevator
The elevator to the viewing gallery of the tower won a design award in 1999. Oddly enough, its space-age design works harmoniously with the stony surroundings. It also permits wheelchair access to the top of the tower – a rare consideration in Prague.

8. Viewing Gallery
The parapet under the Old Town Hall's roof affords visitors a unique view of the square and Staré Město below. A little pocket change will buy you two minutes on a miniature telescope, with which you can admire the Prague Valley.

9. Gothic Cellars
The cellars of the Old Town Hall were once ground-floor rooms. The town was subject to flooding, so more earth was added to keep the burghers' feet dry. The spaces were used as granaries as well as debtors' prisons.

10. The Green
The Old Town Hall's north wing was severely damaged in an urban fight between the Germans and the Czechs during World War II. After the war, the wing was torn down. Now there is a quiet area with benches to sit and escape the crowds.

BUILDING THE OLD TOWN HALL

TOP 10
FEATURES OF THE
ASTRONOMICAL CLOCK

1. Solar clock
2. Lunar clock
3. Josef Mánes Calendar
4. Apostles
5. Angel and the Sciences
6. Vanity, Avarice, Death and Lust
7. Rooster
8. Hourly shows
9. Mikuláš of Kadaň
10. Dial

Prague's Staré Město received its charter and fortifications from John of Luxembourg in 1338, but its town clerk had to wait nearly 150 years for an office. The Old Town Hall was cobbled together from existing houses over the centuries until it comprised the five houses that stand at Staroměstské náměstí 1–2 today. The town hall's eastern wing once stretched to within a few feet of St Nicholas Cathedral (p91), but in 1945 German artillery bombardment reduced it to rubble. The 69.5-m (228-ft) tower was built in 1364, and in 1410 the imperial clockmaker Mikuláš of Kadaň created the basic mechanism of the Prague Orloj, or Astronomical Clock. In 1552 Jan Táborský was put in charge, and by 1566 the clock was fully mechanized.

The Astronomical Clock on the Old Town Hall

CHARLES BRIDGE

J4 Karlův Most

The spectacular Charles Bridge (*Karlův most*) has witnessed battles, executions and, increasingly, film shoots. Architect Petr Parléř built it in Gothic style to replace its predecessor, the Judith Bridge. The bridge's most distinguishing feature is its gallery of 30 statues. The religious figures were installed from 1683 onwards to lead people back to the church. Today all the statues are copies, with the originals in museums.

1 Calvary

This statue will cause double-takes among students of Hebrew. According to a nearby apologia, the words "Holy, holy, holy is the Lord of Hosts" were added in 1696, paid for by a local Jewish man who had been accused of profaning the cross.

2 Old Town Bridge Tower

This beautiful Gothic tower, designed by Petr Parléř (*p27*), was built at the end of the 14th century. Visitors can climb the 138 stairs to the viewing gallery for a jaw-dropping panoramic view of the city.

3 The Lorraine Cross

Midway across the bridge is a brass cross where St John of Nepomuk's body was thrown into the river. It is said that wishes made at the cross will come true.

4 Statue of St John of Nepomuk

At the base of the statue of St John is a brass relief showing a man diving into the river. Rubbing it to attract good luck is an old local tradition; petting the adjacent brass dog is a new one.

5 Statue of Sts Cyril and Methodius

Greek missionaries who brought both Christianity and the Glagolitic alphabet to the Czech and Slovak lands, Cyril and Methodius are revered figures in both countries to this day.

6 Statue of Bruncvik

Peer over the bridge's southern edge to see the Czech answer to King Arthur. Bruncvik, a mythical Bohemian knight, is said to have had a magical sword and helped a lion fight

Clockwise from right Calvary sculpture featuring the crucifix; statue of St John of Nepomuk; bronze relief depicting the martyrdom of St John of Nepomuk

a seven-headed dragon. He and his army are promised to awaken and save Prague at the city's most desperate hour.

7 Our Lady of the Mangles

The portrait of Mary hanging on the house south of the bridge is tied to an ancient tale

of miraculous healing. Seeing the light go out on the balcony below is supposedly an omen of imminent death – don't stare too long.

8 Statue of St Luitgard

Matthias Braun's 1710 depiction of a blind Cistercian nun's celebrated vision, in which Christ appeared to her and permitted her to touch his wounds, has a timeless appeal.

9 Malá Strana Bridge Towers

Charles Bridge ends at the stone archway connecting Malá Strana's two bridge towers. The smaller, stockier structure on the left is the Judith Tower, which dates to the 12th century.

Historic Charles Bridge at sunrise

10 Statue of the Trinitarian Order

This religious order was set up to ransom prisoners of war from the Crusades and buy Christians back their freedom.

WHEN TO VISIT CHARLES BRIDGE

During summer, and increasingly year-round, the bridge is well nigh impassable throughout the day, crowded with artists and tourists. It is best seen in the early hours as the sun rises over the Old Town bridge tower. A late evening stroll gives a similarly dramatic view, with the illuminated cathedral and castle looming above.

LORETA

📍 B2 🏠 Loretánské náměstí 7 🕐 10am–5pm daily 🌐 loreta.cz ⭐

At the heart of this sparkling 17th-century Baroque pilgrimage site is its claim to fame and most proud possession: a replica of the original Santa Casa in Loreto, Italy, believed to be the house where the Virgin Mary received the Incarnation. Construction of the church and the surrounding chapels coincided with the Counter-Reformation, and was intended to lure Czechs back to the Catholic faith.

1 Loretánské náměstí

This historic square is said to have originally been a pagan burial ground. The elegant stucco façade of Loreta is dwarfed by the Černín Palace opposite, home of the Ministry of Foreign Affairs.

2 Santa Casa

The beautiful stucco reliefs on the exterior of this replica of the Holy Family's house in Nazareth depict scenes from the life of the Virgin Mary. Inside stands the miracle-working statue of Our Lady of Loreto.

3 Bell Tower

The carillon was the gift of a merchant of Prague whose daughter was healed by the intercession of the Lady of Loreto.

4 Inner Courtyard

In this courtyard, visitors can admire two Baroque fountains. The south fountain depicts the Assumption of the Virgin; the north

Exquisite ceiling frescoes in the church

Loreta Floorplan

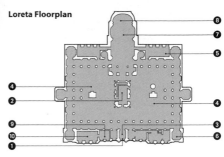

Loreta's Baroque church complex features a sculpture of the Resurrection.

5 Arcade

Before and after visiting the Santa Casa, pilgrims passed through the arcade and prayed at its chapels dedicated to the Holy Family, the Holy Rood, St Francis Seraphim, St Antony of Padua, St Anne and Our Lady of Sorrows.

6 St Wilgefortis Altar

The Chapel of Our Lady of Sorrows contains the altar of a bearded, cruci-fied woman. Wilgefortis was said to be a maiden who prayed for a mascu-line appearance in order to preserve her chastity.

7 Church of the Nativity

Originally a small alcove behind the Santa Casa, the church was expanded into its present size in 1717. The Rococo organ stands opposite the altar, over a crypt to Loreta benefactors.

8 Altars of Sts Felicissimus and Marcia

On either side of the altar in the Church of the Nativity are large reliquary displays con-taining the remains of these two Spanish saints.

9 Prague Sun

The silver monstrance for displaying the host – created in 1699 by Johann Bernard Fischer von Erlach – is gold-plated and studded with 6,222 diamonds.

Diamond-encrusted Prague Sun

The Virgin looks up at her son, represented by the host in the receptacle.

10 Treasury

The Communists created this exhibit of sacred items to show how the papal church brought peasants to obedience with a "cheap promise of happiness beyond the grave".

SANTA CASA

The Santa Casa was the house in Nazareth in which the archangel Gabriel is believed to have announced to the Virgin Mary that she would conceive the Son of God. In the 13th century, the Greek Angeli family moved the house to Loreto, Italy. Copies of the Italian Loreto started emerging all over Europe – the 17th-century Prague site is believed to be the truest representation of the original structure.

THE JEWISH MUSEUM

Ⓦ jewishmuseum.cz ☑

Prague's magnificent Jewish Museum encompasses not just one building but many: four synagogues, the Old Jewish Cemetery, Ceremonial Hall and Robert Guttmann Gallery. Admission to all sites is covered by a single ticket, available from the Visitor Centre or online. Though not formally part of the museum, admission includes the Old-New Synagogue, Europe's oldest surviving synagogue.

1 Visitor Centre

🏛 Maiselova 38/15
🕐 Nov–Mar: Hours vary, check website

Start your visit at the Visitor Centre, where you will find information on each of the museum's sites along with ticket and reservation options.

2 Klausen Synagogue

The museum's largest synagogue (p114) was built in grand Baroque style in 1694 and houses exhibitions that focus on Jewish traditions and culture, which includes family rituals connected to birth, circumcision and marriage. The synagogue is currently undergoing reconstruction work but will reopen in 2025.

3 Pinkas Synagogue

Originally a private prayer house, this 15th-century Gothic structure (p114) is today home to the highly moving "Wall of Commemoration" and an equally emotional exhibition showcasing drawings created by children held at the Nazi-run Terezín (Theresienstadt) ghetto during World War II.

4 Wall of Commemoration

Located within the Pinkas Synagogue (p114), this memorial wall is a beautiful tribute to an estimated 80,000 Czech and Moravians victims of the Holocaust, whose remains could not be returned for burial.

ROBERT GUTTMANN

Prague painter Robert Guttmann (1880–1942) was as much known for his art as for his eccentric appearance and ambitious treks on foot around Europe. In October 1941, the Nazis transported Guttman on the first bus to the Jewish ghetto in Łódź, Poland, where he died six months later.

5 Robert Guttmann Gallery

Named for painter Robert Guttmann, this gallery hosts a collection of works by Guttman along with temporary exhibitions on Jewish history and culture. Be sure to consult the museum website to see what's on.

6 Ceremonial Hall

The ornate Ceremonial Hall (p114) was once the home of Prague's Burial Society, a religious

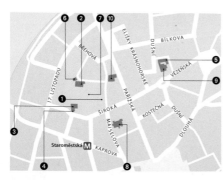

Stunning Moorish interior of the Spanish Synagogue

institution in the ghetto, and many of the rooms were used for parts of the funeral process. Today, it houses an exhibition that covers the society and features artifacts that include ritual objects and memorial prayers.

7 Old Jewish Cemetery

The crumbling Old Jewish Cemetery *(Starý židovský hřbitov)* was one of the few burial sites available to Prague's Jews. Space was so limited that graves had to be layered when the plot was full. Around 12,000 headstones are visible, dating from 1439 to 1787, with hundreds of thousands buried below.

8 Maisel Synagogue

The private synagogue *(p114)* of the 16th-century mayor of the Jewish Quarter and wealthy benefactor, Mordechai Maisel, today it has a permanent exhibition on Jewish history in the Czech Republic from the 10th to 18th centuries.

9 Spanish Synagogue

Richly decorated inside and out, this Moorish style synagogue from the mid-19th century is the most recent addition to the Jewish Quarter. The synagogue *(p113)* houses a continuation of the Maisel Synagogue's exhibition, with the story of local Jewish life in the 19th and 20th centuries.

10 Old-New Synagogue

This evocative synagogue *(p114)* is one of the city's oldest Gothic structures and is still a working synagogue today. Among the highlights are Rabbi Loew's chair; 12 windows of the nave, which evoke the 12 tribes of Israel; and the ark housing sacred Torah scrolls.

Outside the Old-New Synagogue

Old Jewish Cemetery

1. Avigdor Kara's Grave
The oldest grave is that of this poet and scholar, known for his documentation of the pogrom of 1389, which he survived.

2. Mordechai Maisel's Grave
Mordechai Maisel (1528–1601), the mayor of the Jewish ghetto during the reign of Rudolf II, funded the synagogue (p114) that bears his name.

3. Klausen Synagogue
Mordechai Maisel also commissioned the building of the Klausen Synagogue (p114) on the cemetery's northern edge. It now houses exhibitions (p36) on Jewish festivals and traditions.

4. Gothic Tombstones
The eastern wall has fragments of Gothic tombstones rescued from another graveyard near Vladislavova street in 1866. Further graves at another site were found in the 1990s.

5. Hendl Bassevi's Grave
This elaborate tombstone (below) marks the resting place of the "Jewish Queen", Hendl Bassevi. Her husband, mayor Jacob Bassevi, was raised to the nobility by Ferdinand II and permitted a coat of arms, which can be seen on his wife's gravestone.

Tombstone of Hendl Bassevi

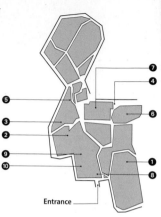

Old Jewish Cemetery Site Map

6. Nephele Mound
Stillborn children, miscarried babies and other infants who died under a year old were buried in the southeast corner of the cemetery.

7. Grave of Rabbi Judah Loew
The grave of Rabbi Judah Loew ben Bezalel (p114), to whom legend attributes the creation of the Prague Golem (p60), is located here.

8. David Gans's Tombstone
Gans's headstone is marked with a goose and the Star of David, after his name and his faith. A pupil of Loew, Gans (1541–1613) was the author of a two-volume history of the Jewish people and an accomplished astronomer during the time of Johannes Kepler.

9. Grave of Rabbi Oppenheim
Rabbi David Oppenheim was the first chief rabbi of Moravia, and later chief rabbi of Bohemia and finally of Prague, where he died in 1736.

10. Zemach Grave
The gravestone of the printer Mordechai Zemach (d 1592) and his son Bezalel (d 1589) lies next to the Pinkas Synagogue (p114). Mordechai Zemach was a co-founder of the Prague Burial Society.

PRAGUE'S JEWISH COMMUNITY

Prague's Jewish community has been integral to the development of the city. Prominent Jewish people, like Rabbi Loew (p114) and Mordechai Maisel paved the way for Jewish participation in the National Revival of the 19th century. In the 20th century, the works of Jewish author Franz Kafka (p56) reached global fame – today, the Kafka Museum is one of the city's biggest draws. However, since arriving in the 10th century, Prague's Jewish community has been continuously subject to anti-Semitism. Pogroms such as the infamous Passover slaughter of 1389 – in which 3,000 Jewish people were killed – have devastated the community. Violence has persisted over the centuries. Notably, the 1899 trial of Leopold Hilsner (a Jewish man accused of ritual murder) began an anti-Jewish campaign in the city. Support for Hilsner from Tomáš Garrigue Masaryk, future President of Czechoslovakia, helped sway public opinion to some degree. In 1939, after the Nazis occupied Prague, the Jewish population was systematically deported to concentration camps. By the end of the war, nearly 80,000 Jewish people from Bohemia and Moravia had died in the Holocaust; Prague's Jewish population has never fully recovered.

Former Jewish ghetto of Staré Město in the early 20th century

ST AGNES OF BOHEMIA CONVENT

◉ M1 ◨ U Milosrdných 17 ◷ 10am–6pm Tue–Sun ⅏ ngprague.cz ◈

The 13th-century St Agnes of Bohemia Convent (*Klášter sv. nežky Ceské*) is a Gothic building closely tied to Czech statehood. Daughter of Czech King Přemyšl Ottokar I, Princess Agnes founded a convent here in 1234 for the Poor Clares, an order of nuns associated with the Order of St Francis. Restored in the 1980s, the convent is now part of the National Gallery and exhibits medieval and early Renaissance art.

1 Strakonice Madonna

This larger-than-life, 700-year-old statue of the Virgin and Child is the Czech National Gallery's most prized possession. The gestures of the Madonna are strikingly rigid, and evoke the Classical French sculpture found in places such as Reims Cathedral.

2 Zbraslav Madonna

Bohemia's most celebrated Marian painting is evocative of Byzantine icons in its style. The ring on the Madonna's left-hand finger symbolizes the church through the mystical marriage between Christ and the Virgin Mary. The work was moved to the St Agnes of Bohemia Convent from the Cistercian Zbraslav Monastery where the majority of the Přemyslid kings were laid to rest.

3 Vyšší Brod Altarpiece

The 14th-century cycle begins with the Annunciation, then proceeds through the Adoration of the Magi to Pentecost. The creator of these beautiful panels is unknown.

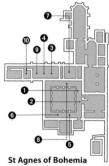

St Agnes of Bohemia Convent Floorplan

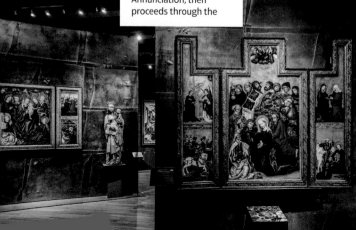

Clockwise from below right
**Gothic exterior of the
convent; the 14th-century
Zbraslav Madonna painting;
Velhartice altarpiece**

4 Works of Master Theodoricus
Parts of an altar set
on loan from Karlštejn
Castle, these works
include *St Charlemagne*,
St Catherine, *St Matthew*,
St Luke, *St Ambrose*
and *St Gregory*.

5 Puchner Altarpiece
St Agnes gave up a
life at court to pursue
a spiritual vocation.
On this 15th-century
altarpiece, she is
typically depicted
nursing the sick.

6 Třeboň Altarpiece
Only three of the
five panels of the
14th-century retable
Třebon Altarpiece

**Medieval art from
the National Gallery**

have survived to
the present day.

7 Capuchin Cycle
The origin of these
fascinating 14 painted
panels is unknown. The
Virgin Mary is flanked by
St Peter on the left and
Christ on the right

8 Velhartice Altarpiece
Originating in south
Bohemia around 1500,
this is a rare example
of a completely
preserved altar.

9 Martyrdom of St Florian
Albrecht Altdorfer
created this painting
as part of a multipanel
altar featuring scenes
from the legend of
St Florian. Other pieces
from the series are
in Florence.

10 Apocalypse Cycle
Although Albrecht
Dürer is considered
the foremost German
Renaissance artist, he is
known to many for his
woodcuts, which date
from 1498 and retain a
strong Gothic flavour.

ST AGNES OF BOHEMIA

St Agnes of Bohemia
was a powerful figure
in medieval politics.
Gregory IX granted
her convent special
privileges. Agnes
died in 1282, but her
influence on Czech
statehood was felt
in 1989, when Pope
John Paul II canonized
her; five days later, the
Velvet Revolution
(p11) began.

8

WENCESLAS SQUARE

📍 N6 🏛 Nové Město

This former medieval horse market began to be redeveloped in the 19th century, rapidly becoming the commercial hub of Prague. In 1848 it was renamed Wenceslas Square (*Václavské náměstí*) in honour of Bohemia's patron saint. The majority of the buildings seen today date from the early 20th century, and have beautiful Art Nouveau façades.

1 National Museum

Invading Warsaw Pact troops shelled the Neo-Renaissance building (*p44*) in 1968, mistaking it for the country's parliament. The entry fee is worth it, if only to see the grand marble stairway and pantheon of Czech cultural figures.

2 St Wenceslas Statue

The Přemyslid prince sits astride a horse flanked by other Czech patrons in Josef Myslbek's 1912 sculpture. The area "under the tail" is a traditional meeting place for locals.

3 Communist Memorial

In front of St Wenceslas is a memorial to the victims of Communism, such as the two men who

>
> **EAT**
> There are cafés, restaurants and shops lined up on both sides of Wenceslas Square from top to bottom. Visit any of these for a delicious meal.

Imposing National Museum building

Prague's bustling
Wenceslas Square

died protesting against
the 1968 invasion.

4 Palác Koruna
Built in 1912 in
Geometric Modernist
style, this "palace"
held offices, homes
and Turkish-style baths.
The listed building now
hosts the Koruna Palace
shopping centre, which
has several cafés and
luxury stores.

5 Palác Lucerna
Václav Havel's
grandfather designed
and built this building,
now home to an art
gallery, cinema, cafés,
shops and a ballroom.

6 Grand Hotel Evropa
Built between 1903 and
1906, this Art Nouveau
building is an architec-
tural gem. The interior is
closed for renovation, but
its beautifully preserved
façade can still be seen.

7 Upside-Down Statue
Hanging in the central
passage of the Palác
Lucerna is David Černý's
take (p68) on Czech
patron saint Wenceslas.

8 Franciscan Garden
A stone's throw from the
busy Wenceslas Square,
this former monastery
garden (p119) provides
much-needed peace
from the city bustle.

9 Church of Our Lady of the Snows
Founded by Charles IV
upon his coronation

Mosaic, Church of
Our Lady of the Snows

in 1347, this beautiful
church was supposed
to have been more than
100 m (330 ft) long, but
it was never completed.

10 Crisis Fallout Shelter
Hidden under the Hotel
Jalta, on the square, is a
nuclear bunker, built in
1953 for high-ranking
officials in the so-called
"Stalin's Baroque" style.
It is now part of the Cold
War Museum (en.muzeum
-studene-valky.cz).

HISTORIC DEMONSTRATIONS

Wenceslas Square
saw its first demon-
stration in 1419 when
Catholic reformer Jan
Želivský led a proces-
sion to St Stephen's
Church. On 28 October
1918 the area wit-
nessed Czechoslovak
independence. In
1969, student Jan
Palach set himself on
fire here as a political
protest against the
Soviet occupation.

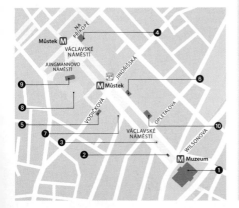

9

NATIONAL MUSEUM

🅶 G5 📍 Václavské náměstí 68 🕐 10am–6pm daily 🌐 nm.cz 🎫📷

The National Museum (*Národní muzeum*) is one of the city's most remarkable buildings and a glimmering repository of cultural and natural artifacts. The museum was conceived in the 19th century as a grand expression of Czech national identity. These days, the museum is housed in two separate buildings linked by a tunnel, and features the country's preeminent collections of natural and ethnographic history.

Exhibition of various minerals

1 Entrance Hall
You can't fail to notice the Neo-Renaissance interiors of the stunning entrance. The highlight is the grand stairway, but you'll find marble pillars, elaborate frescoes and a shimmering glass ceiling with dizzying views up to the cupola.

2 History Exhibition
Seven halls on the main building's first floor are devoted to this sprawling display of historical artifacts, which recounts major historical events from the early medieval period (8th century) to the start of World War I.

3 Halls of Minerals
The first floor is home to a grand exhibition of 4,000 minerals as well as impactites, meteorites and tektites (glass-like debris formed during a meteorite impact). A great place for budding geologists to geek out.

4 Windows into Prehistory
Fossils and models of prehistoric animals are spread out over four rooms on the first floor. Look out for an eye-popping model of the Czech Republic's only native dinosaur, the Burianosaurus.

5 Pantheon
Magnificent intricate busts of famous Czech scholars, writers and artists stand below the cupola on the main building's second floor.

6 Miracles of Evolution
The long story of evolution is recounted through lively exhibits on the second floor of the

main building, stuffed with life-sized models of creatures from the animal kingdom, including a white shark and a 17-m- (55-ft-) long giant squid.

7 Cupola (Dome)
Unafraid of heights? Ride the lift up to the soaring dome for magical views over the city. In the

Ornate interior of the museum

TOP TIP

On the first Monday of every month, entry to both sites of the museum is free.

distance, you can see the spires of Prague Castle.

8 Moments of History

Descend to the underground corridor that links the main building with its annex. An innovative multimedia exhibition projected on the walls traces the history of the city from pre-history to the present.

9 Children's Museum

The museum is a haven for curious young minds. Occupying the second floor of the annex are three halls filled with interactive games and exhibits that can teach little ones about subjects from natural selection to Prague's role in WWII.

10 History of the 20th Century

A bewildering multimedia exhibition on the annex's fourth floor continues Prague's story, from the start of World War I through to the collapse of communism in 1989 and beyond.

BULLET HOLES

The main building is so illustrious that invading Soviet troops in August 1968 mistook it for Czechoslovakia's parliament and riddled the front exterior with bullets, which remained visible despite Communist attempts to cover them up. The building was renovated in the 2010s, but if you look closely, you can still see faint imprints where the bullets struck the façade.

10

PETŘÍN HILL

📍 B4 Ⓜ Malá Strana

Covered with forests and orchards, Petřín Hill is a soft counterpoint to the spires of Hradčany on the Vltava's left bank. Rising more than 300 m (1,000 ft) above sea level, the area began life as a vineyard in the 15th century, but has been a public park since 1825. This park is the perfect place to take a break from the city – stroll along old pathways or take the funicular to see the sights atop the hill.

1 Observation Tower

Modelled after the Eiffel Tower in Paris, Petřín Hill's 63.5-m (210-ft) Eiffelovka stands only one-quarter as high as its inspiration. The tower was created for the Jubilee Exposition of 1891. A climb of 299 stairs leads to the viewing platform.

2 Strahov Stadium

This stadium is the largest arena of its kind in the world. Built for Sokol, a physical exercise organization, it was used for gymnastic rallies. Today it is a rock concert venue.

 EAT
Nebozízek restaurant, situated right in the middle of Petřín Park, offers delicious food along with spectacular views of Petřín Hill and its surroundings.

Onion-domed towers, Church of St Lawrence

3 Strahov Monastery

Founded in 1140, Strahov houses the nation's oldest books in the Strahov Library while still functioning as a monastery. The Theological Hall, with its frescoes and statue of St John, is a must-see.

4 Hunger Wall

The 14th-century wall was once part of the city's southern fortifications. Charles IV is said to have ordered its construction as a project to feed the poor during a famine.

5 Mirror Maze

After laughing at the distorting mirrors in the labyrinth (p71), take in a bit of history with a diorama depicting the last major military action of the Thirty Years' War on Charles Bridge. On the roof of the maze, there are weather vanes with the

Observation Tower on Petřín Hill

names of the workers who worked on the construction in 1891.

6 Church of St Lawrence

This onion-domed church was built on a pagan shrine in the 10th century and rebuilt in Baroque style in the 18th century.

7 Karel Hynek Mácha Statue

Mácha is a national poet, best loved for his Romantic poem "May". On 1 May, admirers lay flowers at his statue.

8 Štefánik's Observatory

Operating since 1928, the observatory was named after M R Štefánik, a Slovak diplomat, scientist and astronomer and the co founder of the Czechoslovak Republic.

9 Kinský Summer Palace

On the Smíchov side of Petřín Hill, this 19th-century palace

houses the National Museum's ethno-graphic collections.

10 Funicular

Do as visitors have done since 1890 and take the funicular railway to the top of the hill and walk down. The cable car offers outstanding views of the castle to the north.

Funicular heading to the top of the hill

TOP 10 OF EVERYTHING

Handpainted Easter eggs

PLACES OF WORSHIP

1 Loreta
At the heart of this elaborate shrine to the Virgin Mary is the Santa Casa – a reproduction of the house where Mary received the Angel Gabriel. Loreta's treasury (p35) holds several priceless monstrances and other artifacts.

2 St Vitus Cathedral
The current building, looming majestically over the castle complex, is a combination of architectural styles and took almost 600 years to complete. In days of old, the cathedral (p26) was the setting for spectacular Bohemian coronations conducted by Prague's archbishops. It is also the final resting place of the saints John of Nepomuk and Wenceslas, as well as scores of other notable Czech figures.

Colourful stained glass, St Vitus Cathedral

3 Old-New Synagogue
Prague's Orthodox Jewish community (p39) still holds services in this 13th-century synagogue (p114), which is the oldest in Central Europe. Its curious name may come from the Hebrew Al-Tenai, meaning "with reservation". Legend has it that its stones will eventually have to be returned to Jerusalem, whence they came.

4 St Nicholas Church, Malá Strana
The Malá Strana church clock tower and dome upstage its namesake across the river. The splendid Baroque sanctuary (p98) was meant to impress Catholic sceptics of the might of Rome.

5 Church of our Lady Victorious
This Baroque church contains the famed statue (p99) of the Infant Jesus of Prague. The wax baby doll is credited with miraculous powers. The resident Order of English Virgins looks after the statue and changes its clothes.

6 Basilica of St James
This is an active place of worship. The Baroque façade (p90) is awash with cherubs and scenes depicting episodes from the lives of saints

Striking Basilica of St James soaring over Prague

Francis of Assisi, James and Antony of Padua. There is also a mummified arm hanging above the door inside.

7 Church of Our Lady before Týn

🗺 M3 🏛 Staroměstské náměstí 14 🕙 10am–1pm & 3–5pm Tue–Sat, 10:30am–noon Sun

The Gothic towers of Týn loom over Old Town Square's houses. During the Counter-Reformation, the Jesuits melted down the gold Hussite chalice that stood between the towers and recast it as the Madonna seen today.

8 Pinkas Synagogue

The names of nearly 80,000 Czech victims of the Holocaust (p36) cover the walls of this notable house (p114), which sits adjacent to the Old Jewish Cemetery. The women's gallery was added in the 18th century.

9 Cathedral of Sts Cyril and Methodius

The assassins of Reinhard Heydrich, the Nazi governor of Czechoslovakia, took refuge in this Eastern Orthodox cathedral (p119) along with members of the Czech Resistance. Surrounded by German troops, they took their own lives on 18 June 1942. The Nazis executed Bishop Gorazd, who had sheltered them.

10 Spanish Synagogue

The present Moorish building with its opulent interior (p113) replaced Prague's oldest synagogue after the latter was razed in 1867. The Conservative Jewish community holds services here. It also houses Jewish Museum exhibits, offices and a reference centre.

Stunning interior of the Spanish Synagogue

The remrkable Eiffel Tower lookalike, Petřín Tower

HISTORICAL SITES

1 Vyšehrad
High above the Vltava River sit the atmospheric ruins *(p130)* of Vyšehrad Castle. The complex includes a medieval royal palace as well as Prague's oldest-surviving rotunda and a 17th-century baroque fortress. It's also home to an ornate Art Nouveau cemetery that features the graves of a roster of Czech writers, artists and composers.

2 Powder Gate
The 15th-century Powder Gate *(p89)* was once the ornate entryway into Prague's Staré Město. The gate marked the start of the coronation route of Bohemian kings – as such, its design features lavish ornamentation and intricate late-Gothic detailing rather than any useful defensive practicalities.

3 Old Town Bridge Tower
Attached to one of the most iconic bridges in the world, the Charles Bridge, this 14th-century Gothic tower *(p32)* is a beloved site in Prague. The tower has borne witness to the high and lows of Czech history, and still bears visible damage received during the Thirty Years War, when marauding Swedish forces attacked the city.

4 Petřín Tower
Originally a lookout tower built for the Prague Jubilee Exhibition of 1891, this remarkable steel structure rises up from the heart of the city *(p46)*. Look familiar? The structure was designed to resemble the Eiffel Tower, so much so that the peak of the tower is the same height as the Eiffel. The 299 steps lead to one of Prague's finest vantage points, with views over the city and beyond.

5 Municipal House (Obecní dům)
This early-20th century cultural centre *(p89)* is a shimmering example of Prague's Art Nouveau architecture and a testament to the talents of a generation of Czech architects and artists,

Medieval Powder Gate at the edge of Staré Město

most notably Alphonse Mucha (1860-1939), the building's designer. Tours explore the splendid interior.

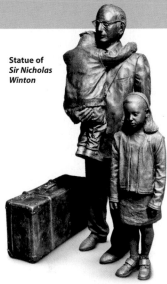

Statue of *Sir Nicholas Winton*

6 Heydrich Terror Memorial

The crypt below the Church of Saints Cyril and Methodius *(p50)* houses two memorials commemorating lives lost during the Nazi occupation. The main memorial honours the seven paratroopers who participated in the assassination of Reinhard Heydrich, Nazi leader in Prague, and died in the church in 1942. The memorials are accompanied by an informative exhibit and video on the occupation years.

7 Sir Nicholas Winton Statue

⚑ H4 ⬥ Wilsonova 300/8
🌐 nicholaswinton.com/memorials

Platform 1 of Prague's Central Station is home to a moving tribute to the man who ran the "Kindertransport" – Sir Nicholas Winton. His work saved the lives of 669 mostly Jewish children, transporting them to safety in the UK prior to World War II. This 2009 bronze statue depicts Winton carrying a little boy and standing next to a young girl.

8 National Memorial on Vitkov Hill

This striking monument *(p129)* to Czechoslovak statehood dates from the 1930s, and has since been subjected to the tides of history. The Nazis destroyed large parts of the monument before the Communists used the the site to bury dignitaries, including their favourite President Klement Gottwald. The site is now owned and maintained by the National Museum, and is home to one of the largest equestrian statues in the world (of Hussite general Jan Žižka).

9 Prague Metronome on Letná Plinth

⚑ E1 ⬥ Letenské sady, Letná

This 23-m- (75-ft-) tall metronome is a remarkable sight in and of itself, designed by sculptor Vratislav Novák as a reminder of time's unceasing flow. But the site's history only enhances its intrigue. It marks the spot where a 15.5-m (51-ft) statue of Soviet dictator Joseph Stalin stood from 1955 to 1962.

10 Žižkov TV Tower

Perennially featured on the "World's Ugliest Buildings" lists, and still evoking mixed feelings among Praguers to this day, this 216-m (709-ft) Communist era tower *(p130)* dominates the city skyline. Built from 1985 to 1992 in the contemporary "high-tech" style, the tower's utilitarian design has since been enlivened by sculptures of ten giant babies by Czech artist David Černý.

MUSEUMS AND GALLERIES

Browsing artworks at the Sternberg Palace

Since 2000, it has also hosted a 19th-century collection. Featured in this collection are French artworks, as well as a splendid collection of Czech modern art. Other locations of the National Gallery are the St Agnes of Bohemia Convent (p40); Sternberg Palace; Schwarzenberg Palace; the Salm Palace and the Kinský Palace (p29).

1 Sternberg Palace

Since 1949, the fine Baroque building of the Sternberg Palace (p105) has been used to house the Prague National Gallery's collection of European art. The gallery is set over three floors that surround the central courtyard. The collection focuses on the Old Masters, and features renowned artists such as Rembrandt, Rubens, El Greco, Van Dyck, Tintoretto and Goya.

2 National Museum

The country's leading natural history and ethnographic museum (p122) is housed in a building that dominates Wenceslas Square. The entrance fee is worth it, if only to see the grand marble stairway, the Pantheon and the interior paintings. The annexe across the street holds rotating exhibitions.

3 Trade Fair Palace

☑ B2 ◩ Dukelských Hrdinů 47 ◷ 10am–6pm Tue–Sun ◫ ngprague.cz ◪

The National Gallery's extensive art collection is spread throughout the city in six locations. It opened its museum of 20th- and 21st-century art in 1995, and is set in a reconstruction of a Trade Fair building from 1928.

4 Smetana Museum

☑ J5 ◩ Novotného lávka 1 ◷ 10am–5pm Wed–Mon ◫ nm.cz ◪

Part of the National Museum, this grand Renaissance-style building, formerly owned by a water company, is a museum dedicated to the father of Czech music, Bedřich Smetana (p56). Documents, letters, scores and instruments detailing his life and work are exhibited here.

5 DOX Centre for Contemporary Art

A multi-functional space located in a former factory, DOX (p130) show-cases unique works of art focusing on current social issues. It also offers special programmes for children.

6 The City of Prague Museum

The collection at this museum (p130) documents the history and cultural development of the Czech capital from prehistory to the 19th century when the Neo-Renaissance building was erected specially for the museum. The exhibition includes china, furniture, relics of medieval guilds, bits of famous buildings and paintings of Prague through the ages. Don't miss Antonín Langweil's

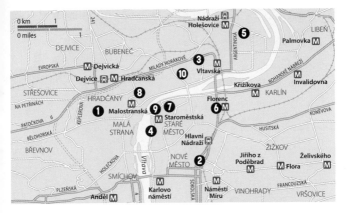

remarkable 1:500 scale model of the city, which is made entirely of paper and wood. It is a snapshot of how the city looked in 1834. The museum also manages 14 other buildings located around Prague that all house exhibitions.

7 Jewish Museum

First opened in 1906, the seven sites that comprise this museum *(p36)* display thousands of personal artifacts, documents and books that detail and preserve Jewish history in Bohemia and Moravia. Each of the seven sites tells a different part of the Jewish story in Prague. The museum also has a fabulous Jewish art collection.

8 Kunsthalle Praha

📍 D1 🏛 Klárov 5 🕐 11am–7pm Thu–Mon, 11am–9pm Wed
🌐 hunsthallepraha.org

Located in the building of the former Zenger transformer station, this cultural and arts space presents contemporary exhibits from Czech and international artists across three galleries. The museum hosts a wide range of short-term exhibitions, educational projects, cultural events and social activities. The design shop offers a diverse selection of limited edition Czech and international design pieces in collaboration with artists.

9 Museum of Decorative Arts

📍 K3 🏛 17 listopadu 2 🕐 10am–8pm Tue 10am–6pm Wed–Sun
🌐 upm.cz ♿

The museum focuses on historical and contemporary crafts, applied arts and design. Its glass collection is one of the largest in the world, but only a fraction of it is ever on display.

10 National Technical Museum

📍 F1 🏛 Kostelní 42 🕐 9am–6pm Tue–Sun 🌐 ntm.cz ♿

This is the ultimate how-things-work museum, with exhibitions on everything from mining and metallurgy to transport and astronomy. Ask a guide to show you the coal mine.

Exhibit at the National Technical Museum

WRITERS AND COMPOSERS

1 Franz Kafka
Although he wrote in German and almost none of his work was published in his lifetime, Franz Kafka *is* Prague. Many of his disturbing novels seem to foresee the Communist years. His work has inspired other Prague artists: look out for the giant rotating Kafka head outside Quadrio shopping centre by David Černý.

2 Božena Němcová
One of the greatest Czech writers of the 19th century, Božena Němcová was a founder of modern Czech prose. She was particularly interested in folklore – her work consists of short stories and more extensive prose against a rural backdrop. She is known for her novella *Babička (The Grandmother)*, regarded as a classic of Czech literature.

3 Karel Čapek
This Czech writer is best known for his science fiction and psychologically penetrating novels. With his 1920 play *R.U.R. (Rossum's Universal Robots)* he gave the world a word for an automaton, from the Czech word *robota*, meaning "forced labour".

Author Karolína Světlá, famous for her novels

4 Karolína Světlá
Born in 1830, Světlá became one of the most prominent Czech authors during the 19th century. She is regarded as the founder of the Czech novel. Many of her books, including *Černý Petříček* and *Zvonečková královna*, depicted life in Prague during the 19th century and focused mainly on societal issues from that time.

Czech author and playwright Karel Čapek

5 Jaroslav Hašek
A notorious joker and the author of the celebrated satirical dig at the Austrian army, *The Good Soldier Švejk* (published in 1921), Hašek was also the creator of the Party for Moderate Progress Within the Bounds of the Law.

6 Bedřich Smetana
The composer wrote his opera *Libuše*, based on the legendary princess, for the reopening of Prague's National Theatre in 1883. Smetana vies

with Antonín Dvořák for the title of best-loved Czech composer; the former's ode to beer in *The Bartered Bride* gives him a certain advantage.

7 Antonín Dvořák

The works of Dvořák, such as his *Slavonic Dances*, regularly incorporate folk music. He composed his final *New World Symphony* while he was director of the National Conservatory in New York City.

8 Bohumil Hrabal

This poetic author used to sit in the Staré Město pub U Zlatého tygra *(p94)*, taking down the stories he heard there. His most notable works are *Closely Watched Trains*, *I Served the King of England* and *Too Loud a Solitude*.

9 Květa Legátová

A writer and novelist, Legátová is known for *Želary*, a collection of short stories that explore the harsh reality of early 20th-century life in a remote fictional Czech village. In 2002, she was awarded the State Prize for Literature and published *Jozova Hanule*, her autobiographical novel.

10 Václav Havel

The former Czech president was known as a playwright and philosopher before he became a civil rights activist protesting the Warsaw Pact invasion in 1968 *(p10)*. His absurdist works and fame helped draw international attention to the struggles of his country.

Former Czech president Václav Havel

TOP 10 WORKS OF ART, MUSIC AND LITERATURE

1. Slav Epic
Art Nouveau master Alfons Mucha celebrates the Czech mythic past in this cycle of 20 large canvases.

2. The Castle
Kafka worked on this novel of social alienation while living in Prague Castle's Golden Lane *(p23)*.

3. The Good Soldier Švejk
Hašek was so effective in making fun of the army and the Austro-Hungarian empire that Czechs still have a hard time taking authority seriously.

4. Home Cook
At the start of the 19th century, M D Rettigová became a pioneer in the field of culinary literature with this book.

5. R.U.R.
Karel Čapek's science-fiction play is a sometimes dark study of labour relations and social structures.

6. The Grandmother
Author Božena Němcová based the narrator in her 1855 novella *Babička* on her own grandmother, from whom she heard many of these stories.

7. Vltava
Smetana's *Má vlast (My Homeland)* is a set of six tone or symphonic poems celebrating Bohemia. The second, *Vltava*, follows the eponymous river's course.

8. New World Symphony
With his ninth symphony, composed in 1893, Dvořák incorporated the style of American folk songs.

9. Disturbing the Peace
Havel meditates on Communism and the values underlying Central Europe's pursuit of democracy in this work.

10. The Unbearable Lightness of Being
The novel is Milan Kundera's non-linear tale of love, politics and the betrayals inherent in both.

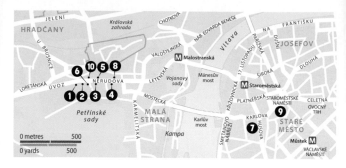

HOUSE SIGNS

1 The White Swan
🏠 Nerudova 49

Prague houses weren't given identifying numbers until 1770, when Empress Maria Theresa brought the famed Habsburg trait of orderliness from Vienna to the banks of the Vltava. Before that, homes were known and located by a charming but confusing system of allegorical symbols. Nerudova street in Malá Strana (p96) has the highest concentration of house signs in the city. Originally many of them had local significance, although today much of their meaning has been lost. The White Swan is one of these, and probably originated as a golden goose.

2 The Two Suns
🏠 Nerudova 47

This house was once the home of the much-loved Czech poet and author Jan Neruda (1834–91), after whom

The Two Suns house sign

the street is named. Traditionally, this was the writers' and artists' area of Prague, and Neruda conveyed the Bohemian atmosphere of Malá Strana in his work. The connection continues today with the quarter's many small art galleries and craft shops.

3 The Golden Key
🏠 Nerudova 27

Castle goldsmiths, such as the ones who worked at this house in the 17th century, paid fees to the city, unlike their colleagues who lived in the castle's Golden Lane (p23). As such, they were entitled to advertise their wares, as preserved today in this building's façade.

4 The Red Lamb
🏠 Nerudova 11

One of the street's more unlikely symbols, the scarlet sheep adorning this façade has a significance so arcane, not even the current house owner can explain it. It remains in place as one of the city's many idiosyncrasies.

5 The Golden Wheel
🏠 Nerudova 28

This house symbol may have had something to do with alchemy – the wheel represents a stage in the *magnum opus*, the process by which the base metal lead was purportedly turned into gold.

6 The Green Lobster
📍 Nerudova 43

Who knows what they were thinking when they hung the crustacean above their door – probably trying to keep up with the neighbours at the Pendant Parsnip (No 39).

7 Golden Tiger
📍 Husova 17

This 15th-century house was originally decorated with a hoe, but this was changed in 1702 to a mural of a golden tiger, which still stands above the door. Most famously it was the favourite pub of the Czech author Bohumil Hrabal.

8 The Three Fiddles
📍 Nerudova 12

They say a demonic trio screeches on their instruments here on moon-lit nights. The house was home to a family of violin-makers in the early 18th century, and the sign advertised their trade. Like many of the other buildings on this street, it is now home to a restaurant.

9 St Wenceslas's Horse
📍 Staroměstské náměsti 16

This mural can be seen on the façade of Štorch House (also

Mural of St Wenceslas on horseback, Štorch House

referred to as "At the Stone Virgin Mary") located at the Old Town Square (p28). Created by Mikoláš Aleš, it acts as a tribute both to the patron saint of Bohemia and the blacksmiths who shod horses bound for the castle.

10 The Golden Horseshoe
📍 Nerudova 34

The ornate doorway of this beautiful pale-blue building is adorned with an image of St Wenceslas on horseback. Below this dangles a golden horseshoe; it's likely that this was once the home or workshop of a blacksmith.

Beautiful doorway of the Golden Horseshoe

MYTHS AND LEGENDS

**Representation of
the Golem**

1 The Golem
It is said that rabbi Judah Loew
(p114) created a clay automaton to
defend the Jews of the Prague ghetto.
When the creature ran amok one day,
Loew was forced to deactivate him
and stash him in the attic of the Old-
New Synagogue *(p114)*.

2 Turk in Ungelt
Among the merchants who
lived in the Týn settlement behind
the Church of Our Lady *(p51)* was
a Turkish immigrant. When his
betrothed ran off and married
another, he flew into a rage and
chopped her head off. He is said
to wander around the Ungelt
courtyard carrying the
decapitated head.

3 One-Armed Thief
The story of the thief who sought
to steal jewels from a statue of the
Madonna in the Basilica of St James *(p90)*,
claims that the stony Virgin seized him
by the arm and local butchers had to
cut him loose. According to some, the
thief still haunts the church asking
visitors to help him fetch his arm.

**4 Ghosts and
Legends Museum**
 D3 Mostecká 18
 mysteriapragensia.cz
Uncover old Prague's most famous
mysteries and legends in this museum
exploring the city's ghosts and stories.
The cellar has a replica of some of old
Prague's streets, while the ground floor
offers more traditional exhibits that
provide background to the legends.

5 The Iron Man
Falsely believing his fiancée to
be unfaithful, a knight called off their
wedding. After she drowned herself
in grief, he realized his mistake and
hanged himself. Every 100 years he
appears in Platnéřská street to find
a young virgin who will free him by
talking to him for at least an hour.

6 The Drowned Man
In the late 19th century, young
Bobeř Říma stole a bicycle and rode it
into the river. If a soggy fellow tries to
sell you a bike near the Staré Město end
of Charles Bridge, just keep walking.

**A woodcut (1512) depicting
a werewolf attack**

7 Werewolf

Apparently, the gamekeeper of Rudolf II became so enamoured with the wolves that roamed the castle's Stag Moat that he became one himself. Nowadays, he takes the form of a large dog and tends to chase cyclists, joggers and tourists when the whim takes him, so keep looking over your shoulder.

8 Emmaus Devil

In an attempt to bedevil the monks at the Emmaus Monastery (p121), Satan worked there as a cook and laced the monks' food with pepper and other spices. To this day, Czech cuisine has few piquant flavours.

9 Drahomíra

St Wenceslas's mother was, by all accounts, an unpleasant woman. She killed her mother-in-law and might have done in her son, too, but it is said that the gates of hell swallowed her up before she could act. She sometimes wheels through Loretánská náměstí in a fiery carriage.

10 The Mad Barber

When a local barber forsook his home and family after he became caught up in alchemical pursuits, his daughters ended up in a brothel and his wife killed herself. He is said to haunt Karlova and Liliova streets, hoping to return to his honest profession and make amends.

**Gothic Charles Bridge
in the evening**

TOP 10 FOLK TALES

1. John of Nepomuk Died on Charles Bridge
Nepomuk was already dead when he was thrown over the side of the bridge by assassins hired by the king, Václav IV(p32).

2. Vyšehrad Castle
While it's true that Vyšehrad (p127) was the first seat of power, its importance has been inflated by legend.

3. Alchemists Lived in Golden Lane
Alchemists tended to live on credit in houses in town during the reign of Emperor Rudolf II.

4. Czechs are Believers
In the 2021 census, over 57 per cent of Czechs identified as not having a religion. Over 30 per cent of the population did not declare.

5. Jan Masaryk Committed Suicide
In 1948 the foreign minister was found dead in front of Černín Palace, having "fallen" from a window, according to the Communists.

6. There's Only One Bud
The Czech town of České Budějovice (Budweis in German) was producing beer before the US brewer, but didn't register its copyright on the name.

7. The Danube Flows through Prague
It's incredible how many visitors think the Danube flows through the Czech capital. The river here is the Vltava.

8. Absinth Will Affect Your Mind
The amount of wormwood in the drink is negligible is not enough to cause negative changes.

9. Czechs and Slovaks are the Same Nation
Despite centuries of shared history and continued affiliation, Czechs and Slovaks have distinct languages, cultures and traditions.

10. Prague is the New Left Bank
After the Velvet Revolution, some proclaimed Prague "the Paris of the 90s", due to the number of expats.

Clockwise from top right
Plain exterior of the towering Basilica of St James; intricate Baroque relief of apostle St Anthony of Padua; stunning frescoes and decoration above the nave of the church

ECCENTRIC PRAGUE

1 Museum of Senses

Challenge your senses at this museum *(p122)*, where nothing is as it seems. Walk through a jungle in a tunnel where the river flows upwards or stand on top of a skyscraper and step into a desert. The amazing optical illusions here create a fun experience for the entire family.

2 Marionette Don Giovanni

Mozart premiered his opera *Don Giovanni* in 1787 at Prague's Estates Theatre *(p73)*. Of the two marionette homages to the city's favourite opera, the better production

takes place at the National Marionette Theatre *(p73)*. The technique of the puppeteers is so masterful, you'll leave looking for strings attached to passersby.

3 Pragulic

🗺 L4 🏠 Staroměstshé náměstí 4
🌐 pragulic.cz

This unusual social enterprise enables you to experience the world from the perspective of homeless people, challenge stereotypes and gain insight into their daily life. Walking tours are organized by guides among the homeless and visitors can choose between short two-hour tours or a 24-hour one.

4 Gallery of Steel Figures

🗺 M4 🏠 Celetná 15
🕐 10am–10pm daily
🌐 galerieocelovychfigurin.cz

At this gallery, enjoy an interactive and original exhibition inspired by more than 100 characters from cartoons, sci-fi or pop culture. The figures here are made from recycled steel parts. There is also a souvenir shop and a café.

Entrance of the National Marionette Theatre

5 Sex Machines Museum

📍 L4 🏛 Melantrichova 18
🕐 10am–11pm daily 🌐 sexmachines
museum.com 🔗

An exhibition in a slightly different sense, this is one show that's definitely not for kids. The museum traces the history of instruments for sexual gratification, from their origins to the modern day. While not entirely without cultural merit, the overall package is rather bizarre.

6 Folimanka Underground Bunker

🏛 Pod Karlovem Street 🕐 Hours vary, chech website 🌐 krytfolimanka.cz

This bunker, with an extensive maze of corridors and rooms, was built during the Cold War as a refuge for civilians in case of any nuclear threat. There's also an exhibition with photos of other civilian bunkers located in Prague. This underground bunker is open to the public once a month on a Saturday.

7 Dripstone Wall

📍 D2 🏛 Wallenstein Garden, Malá Strana 🕐 Apr–Oct: 7am–7pm Mon–Fri, 9am–7pm Sat & Sun; Jun–Sep: 7am–7pm daily

This undeniably eerie wall is on the southeastern edge of the manicured Wallenstein Garden (p83). From afar, it looks like an enormous wall of grey stalactites but, closer, you'll notice haunting features hidden in the wall, from snakes to grotesque human faces.

8 Museum of Torture

📍 M4 🏛 Celetná 12 🕐 10am–10pm daily; winter: 10am–8pm daily 🌐 museumtortury.cz 🔗

If you can't grasp how these grisly instruments work, the illustrations should make their operation painfully clear. About 100 implements of pain and dozens of etchings are on display, along with explanations.

9 McGee's Ghost Tours

📍 M3 🏛 Týnská 21 🌐 mcgees ghosttours.com

Whether you are a believer or a sceptic, the guides can guarantee an entertaining evening as they take you through narrow lanes and cobbled alleys to churches and monuments. Learn about alchemists, murderers and the unfortunate souls who lived here. There are three different guided tours that last three hours each.

10 Idiom

📍 K4 🏛 Municipal Library of Prague, Mariánské náměstí 1 🕐 9am–8pm Tue–Fri, 1–8pm Mon & Sat

Located right by the entrance to the Municipal Library of Prague, this eye-catching art installation consists of 8,000 books in a spiral – although, thanks to some clever mirror placement, it appears to go on forever.

Haunting Dripstone Wall, Wallenstein Garden

Lovely landscaped Wallenstein Garden

PARKS AND GARDENS

1 Petřín Hill
Stroll in the shade of trees and explore all manner of architectural quirks, from a medieval defensive wall to a mini Eiffel Tower, in one of Prague's largest green spaces (p46). In spring the views are at their best when the orchards are in bloom.

2 Vrtba Garden
Arguably the most beautiful in Prague, this Baroque-styled garden (p99) was designed by František Maxmilián Kaňka, who first renovated the palace for Jan Josef, Count of Vrtba, and then created the garden. It is located right behind Vrtba Palace, on the slopes of Petřín Hill (p46).

Baroque Vrtba Garden on Petřín Hill

3 Wallenstein Garden
Albrecht von Wallenstein razed two dozen houses to make way for his expansive "backyard", which features an artificial lake. Among the garden's (p83) stranger elements is the grotto on the south wall, with stalactites imitating a limestone cave. The cries you hear all around you are the resident peacocks.

4 Kampa Island
Kampa Island is a delightfully peaceful corner of Malá Strana. Residents love to sunbathe, sip wine and play frisbee on the island green (p98) in summer. They also like to smoke marijuana, beat drums well into the night and enjoy a relaxed picnic on the island park away from the hustle and bustle of the city.

5 Vyšehrad
Far enough from the centre to be largely tourist-free, Vyšehrad (p127) is the perfect place to be alone with your thoughts. Sights include the Neo-Gothic Sts Peter and Paul Church, the graves of Dvořák and Smetana and reconstructed fortifications. However, visitors should be aware that there's very little shelter from inclement weather.

6 Stromovka

King Přemysl Ottokar II established the royal hunting park here in 1266. A public garden since 1804, Stromovka *(p128)* is one of the city's largest parks. It has four ponds that are ideal for ice-skating in winter and duck-feeding in summer, and meandering paths that offer easy strolling.

7 South Gardens of Prague Castle

The spectacular views of Malá Strana from these castle-skirting gardens *(p22)* won't fail to inspire. Enter via the stairs from the Third Courtyard for a pleasant way to conclude a day of sightseeing in Hradčany.

8 Palace Gardens Below Prague Castle

This historic complex of beautiful interconnected terrace gardens is situated on the southern slopes of the Prague Castle in Malá Strana. The gardens abound in rich architectural decoration, decorative staircases, balustrades, scenic terraces, garden-houses and pavilions.

9 Franciscan Garden

Stop here after pounding the pavements of Wenceslas Square

Singing Fountain in the Royal Garden

and join the pensioners and office workers at lunch, quietly filling the benches behind the Church of Our Lady of the Snows *(p43)*.

10 Prague Castle Royal Garden

These formal gardens were laid out on the orders of the Habsburg king Ferdinand I in 1534 *(p105)*. After admiring Queen Anne's summer palace and the Communist-revised frescoes in the Ball Game Hall, slip down to the Stag Moat *(p106)*.

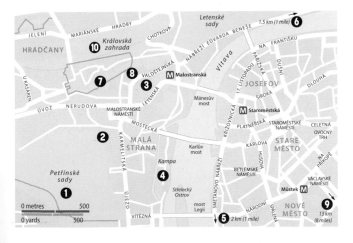

OFF THE BEATEN TRACK

Upside-down horse statue by David Černý

horse in the central passage of the Palác Lucerna is worth a special look and a laugh. It is a gentle parody of the pompous horse statue at the top of Wenceslas Square.

1 David Černý's Upside-Down Horse Statue

📍 N6 🏛 Štěpánská 61 🕐 8am– midnight daily 🌐 lucerna.cz

Works by Czech installation artist David Černý can be seen around the city, but this hanging statue of St Wenceslas astride an upside-down

2 Cubist Lamppost

📍 M6 🏛 Jungmannovo náměstí

The city of Prague was a hotbed of architectural experimentation in the 20th century, enthusiastically embracing the application of Cubist design concepts to all manner of buildings and objects, including – apparently – lampposts. The only one of its kind in the world, this street light can be found on a corner between Václavské náměstí and Jungmannovo náměstí.

3 Fantova Kavárna

📍 H4 🏛 Wilsonova 80 🌐 fantova-havarna.cz

The old part of Prague's main train station, Hlavní nádraží, is a beautiful building. Head upstairs from the grand concourse to admire the opulent 1909 Art Nouveau Fantova

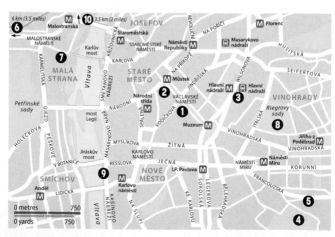

An audio-visual exhibit at the Karel Zeman Museum

Kavárna, named after the station's architect. The ambience and the beautiful interiors of the renovated station can be appreciated while sipping coffee at the café.

4 Grebovka
📍 B6 🏛 Havlíčkovy sady 2188 🕐 10am–10pm daily
🌐 pavilongrebovka.cz

Vinohrady was once covered by vineyards (that's what the name means). This pleasant gazebo in a park south of Náměstí Míru is all that's left, but it is still a wonderful place to spend a sunny afternoon sipping wine in the open air.

5 Krymská
📍 C6 🏛 Vršovice

Prague's hipster scene is thriving along this pleasantly dilapidated street in the district of Vršovice. There are several good cafés and bars, where modern trends and old Prague clash to fascinating effect.

6 Divoká Šárka
📍 A5

This expansive nature reserve offers a touch of wilderness within a short tram ride of the centre. There are rugged rock formations, deep forests and even a refreshing stream-fed swimming pool during the summer months. The hilly meadows are a great spot for kite-flying in autumn.

7 Karel Zeman Museum
📍 D3 🏛 Saský dvůr, Malá Strana 🕐 10am–7pm daily
🌐 muzeumkarlazemana.cz

This interactive museum focuses on the work of renowned Czech filmmaker Karel Zeman, who directed several noteworthy Czech fantasy films, including *The Fabulous World of Jules Verne* and *The Fabulous Baron Munchausen*.

8 Riegrovy Sady
📍 H5

This sprawling park, partly designed in the style of an English garden, offers plenty of room to spread a blanket and admire views out over the Staré Město with Prague Castle in the distance.

9 Náplavka
📍 E6 🏛 Nové Město

The Vltava's eastern bank south of the National Theatre has come into its own as the go-to summer venue, and offers visitors everything from music festivals to farmers' markets.

10 Hotel International
📍 B5 🏛 Koulova 15
🌐 internationalprague.cz

Despite spending 40 years under Communism, central Prague has little architecture to show for it. This impressive Socialist-Realist palace – a 1950s gift from the Soviet Union – is a reminder. Check out the period-piece lobby decor.

A herd of giraffes at the popular Prague Zoo

FAMILY ATTRACTIONS

1 Prague Zoo

Located on a rocky slope north of the centre overlooking the Vltava, the Prague Zoo (p127) was founded in 1924. It is home to more than 5,000 animals representing close to 700 species, 50 of which are extremely rare in the wild. There are 12 pavilions, including Hippo House, Bird Outlands, Elephant Valley and a Children's Zoo.

2 Public Transport Museum

A1 Patočhova 2 9am–5pm Sat & Sun dpp.cz/muzeum-mhd

This museum located in the former Střešovice tram depot celebrates more than 150 years of Prague's transport systems. Exhibits include more than 40 historic vehicles from horse-drawn carriages to various types of trams, buses and maintenance vehicles. Other exhibits include models, photographs, historical documents, tickets, drawings and route maps.

3 Puppet Shows

Puppetry is a long-standing Czech tradition, and late afternoon shows will keep your children entertained for up to an hour. There's enough action that younger folk usually don't mind not understanding the libretto or narration. Weekend presentations of well-known fairy tales at the National Marionette Theatre (p73) can fill up quickly, so book in advance.

4 DinoPark

OC Galerie Harfa Hours vary, check website dinopark.eu

Located on the roof of the Harfa Shopping Centre near Českomoravská metro station, DinoPark is the perfect place for all inquisitive minds. This attraction includes models of static and robotic life-sized dinosaurs, a palaeontological playground for kids, 4D cinema and much more.

5 National Technical Museum

Located in a huge hanger-like hall, this excellent, hands-on museum (p55) is sure to be a hit with kids. Inside there are vintage cars and steam trains to clamber on, a mock coal mine and a working TV studio.

6 Railway Kingdom

B6 Stroupežnického 23, Smíchov 9am–7pm daily railroad-kingdom.com

The miniature world of the Railway Kingdom has dozens of model trains and cars, hundreds of metres of track, replicas of important buildings in the Czech Republic, plus an exhibition which features a unique interactive model of Prague at a 1:1000 scale.

7 Botanical Garden Troja

This garden is spread out over 30 ha (74 acres) and includes the historic vineyards of St Clara, a Japanese meditation garden and the unique tropical greenhouse Fata Morgana. Kids should take the cartoon map and see if they can solve the puzzle by finding 14 interesting plants and affixing stickers of them onto the correct sections.

8 Black Light Theatre
K4 Divadlo Ta Fantastika: Karlova 8

There are many black-light shows at theatres (p72) around the Staré Město, but the best one is at Divadlo Ta Fantastika. The brilliant displays should keep youngsters mesmerized.

9 Boat Trips
While adults might enjoy the old-fashioned rowing boats, children will prefer the splashing, pedalling action of the miniature paddleboats on the Vltava. Numerous vendors rent boats and sell tickets near the National Theatre (p120). Take all the usual precautions to ensure that no one goes overboard.

10 Mirror Maze
The warped mirrors here are great fun for making faces, pointing fingers at elongated bodies and giggling hysterically. For older children interested in a bit of gore and history combined, the battle-scene diorama is another of the many attractions on Petřín Hill (p46).

Inside the fascinating Mirror Maze in Petřín Park

TOP 10
SPECIALITY STORES FOR KIDS

1. Marionettes under the Bridge
U Lužického semináře 7
An assortment of traditional wooden Czech puppets are on offer at this chain.

2. SPARKYS dům hraček Juliš
Václavské náměstí 22
This multi-level store has an excellent selection of toys, games and gifts that will appeal to all kids.

3. Loutky
Nerudova 51
Everything from hand puppets to antique puppets can be found here.

4. Agátín svět
Sokolovská 67, Karlín
Agatha's World offers a range of educational toys for kids of all ages.

5. Hugo chodí bos
Vodičkova 35, Nové Město
This shop has a lot to offer, from classic, locally made Czech toys to educational games.

6. Lego Museum
Národní 31
More megastore than museum, this city centre attraction has toys galore.

7. Kouzelné Hračkářství
Lesnická 6, Smíchov
Magic Toy Shop is a place full of toys, clothes and creative sets for children.

8. Space 4 Kids
Vinohradská 21, Vinohrady
This shop is known for its range of kids furniture sourced from around the world.

9. U Mostu
U Lužického semináře 5
Shop for handmade souvenirs here, made with love and inspired by Prague.

10. Hračky U Zlatého lva
Celetná 32
Find all sorts of toys for little ones including handmade wooden toys, children's puzzles and dolls in traditional folk costumes.

PERFORMING ARTS VENUES

1 State Opera

Set at the top of Wenceslas Square next to the National Museum is the Státní opera (p120). Originally known as the New German Theatre, it was built to rival the National Theatre. It offers a repertoire heavy on Italian and Viennese favourites.

2 Divadlo Archa

P3 ◻ Na Poříčí 26
W divadloarcha.cz

The premiere venue for avant-garde theatre in Prague, Divadlo Archa has hosted artists such as David Byrne and Compagnie Pál Frenák.

3 Hybernia Theatre

P4 ◻ Náměstí Republiky 4
W hybernia.eu

Housed in a former monastery, this theatre opened in 2006 with the musical *Golem*. It hosts a range of cultural events.

4 Ponec

C6 ◻ Husitshá 24a, Žižhov
W divadloponec.cz

This contemporary dance and movement theatre space, opened in 2001, has all aspects covered, from top international dance acts to workshops for young talent.

5 Smetana Hall

P3 ◻ Náměstí Republiky 5
W foh.cz

The glorious Art Nouveau Smetana Hall at the Municipal House is home to the Prague Symphony Orchestra (Fok). Prague Spring Music Festival (p84) traditionally opens here with Smetana's *Má vlast (p57)*.

6 The New Stage

K6 ◻ Národní třída 4
W narodni-divadlo.cz

A variety of themes involving dance, music, pantomime, black light and multimedia projections are used by the actors of Laterna Magika to bring alive stories on the stage.

7 National Theatre

The Národní divadlo curtain first went up for Smetana's *Libuše* in 1883; you can still see this or other Czech operas on the same stage. Go to a performance to appreciate the artistic work that went into creating the theatre (p120).

Neo-Classical façade of the Estates Theatre

8 Estates Theatre

📍 M4 🏛 Ovocný trh 1
🌐 narodni-divadlo.cz

Stavovské divadlo is well known as the venue where Mozart's *Don Giovanni* saw its first performance. It was also the first Czech-language playhouse in what was then a largely German-speaking city. The productions occasionally leave something to be desired, but if you don't see the *Don* here, then where?

9 Rudolfinum

📍 K2 🏛 Alšovo nábřeží 12
🌐 rudolfinum.cz

The Rudolfinum is home to the Czech Philharmonic Orchestra. Between 1918 and 1939, and for a brief period after World War II, the Rudolfinum was the seat of the Czechoslovak Parliament.

10 National Marionette Theatre

📍 L3 🏛 Žatecká 1

The National Theatre's puppet stage represents the pinnacle of this genre, staging wonderful productions of Czech fairy tales and other shows (in Czech). They have the best Beatles tribute in town and a marionette version of *Don Giovanni* (p64).

A performance at the National Theatre

TOP 10 CHURCHES FOR MUSIC RECITALS

1. St Cajetan Church
📍 C2 🏛 Nerudova 22
This magnificent Baroque church regularly holds concerts of Bach, Mozart or Brahms.

2. St Agnes of Bohemia Convent
This medieval convent (p40) regularly holds recitals of classical music.

3. St Nicholas Church, Malá Strana
Appreciate the Malá Strana church's Baroque grandeur (p98) at a concert of sacred music.

4. Basilica of St James
This active house of worship (p90) is famous for its organ concerts and regularly invites the general public to hear the 18th century organ, which includes 8,277 pipes.

5. Mirror Chapel
The Baroque chamber of the Clementinum (p90) hosts string quartets and other small ensembles.

6. St Martin in the Wall
📍 L6 🏛 Martinská 8
This Gothic church was once part of the Staré Město defences. Today the excellent acoustics of the church make this a great place to enjoy organ and other recitals that appear on the bill.

7. Spanish Synagogue
The ornate 1880 organ figures in the classic music concerts held in this opulent synagogue (p113).

8. St George's Basilica
The choral and string recitals here (p23) present the greatest works of Mozart, Beethoven and others.

9. Church of Sts Simon and Jude
📍 L1 🏛 U Milosrdných
Catch an ensemble of the Prague Symphony Orchestra players in this Renaissance sanctuary.

10. St Nicholas Cathedral, Staré Město
The Staré Město church (p91) hosts chamber music recitals daily and performances by the Czech Philharmonic Orchestra.

NIGHTS OUT

Crowds around the bar at the always lively Cross Club

1 Traditional Czech Pubs
Prague is filled with many excellent centuries-old pubs, nearly all of which are home to great beer and good vibes. Get a taste for the city's favourite tipple, Pilsner Urquell, at U Pinkasů (*upinkasu.cz*) or rub shoulders with locals in the historic halls of U Fleků (*en.ufleku.cz*).

2 Cabaret
Be transported back decades by an evening of high-energy artistic cabaret. At Hybernia Theater (*p72*) cabaret, modern circus, vaudeville and burlesque come together in a dazzling display that could rival the Moulin Rouge in Paris.

3 Cellar Bars
Join the locals underground at one of Prague's famous cellar bars. Most bars serve a variety of popular beers but Andělský Pivovar (*andelskypivovar.cz*) brews its own (the brewing vats can be seen inside). Not a beer fan? Then step into Black Angel's Bar (*blackangelsbar.com*) for cocktails and cigars.

4 Theatre
Prague's theatre scene is incredibly vibrant yet often overlooked by visitors. See iconic plays, Czech opera and ballet at the National Theatre (*p120*), or visit the historic Estates Theatre (*p73*) where Mozart debuted his opera *Don Giovanni*. Want something more unusual?

Try "black theatre" at Ta Fantastika Theatre (*tafantastika.cz*) where silent shows use light on a black backdrop to tell stories.

5 Soak in a Beer Spa
Prague loves beer so much that it's now become a therapeutic treatment. No we're not joking, the hops and barley supposedly have health benefits. Still don't believe us? Then head to the Original Beer Spa (*beerspa.com*) and relax in the tubs of hops while you enjoy a glass of the finished product.

6 Ghost Tours
Give yourself a scare and learn of the spooky stories and tall tales that enliven Prague's history. Head down narrow alleys on an immersive evening walking tour with McGee's Ghost Tours (*p65*) or trade ghostly tales for dingy dungeons with Prague Underground Tours (*prague-underground-tours.com*).

7 Swanky Cocktail Bars
Just because Praguers love a beer, doesn't mean they don't also enjoy a cocktail. Sample the classics at the iconic Bukowski's bar (*Bořivojova 689/86*) or discover a weird range of cocktails, including whisky-infused penicillin, at hip Groove Bar (*groovebar.cz*).

8 Night Clubs

There's a club for all in Prague, no matter whether you like a bit of disco, rave or just cheesy classics. The Roxy *(p93)* is a staple and continues to pump out jungle and dub from big-name DJs. M1 Lounge *(m1lounge.com)*, meanwhile, is the place to be for RnB, both modern and old-school.

9 Live Music

Every night, Prague throbs to the sound of live music of every genre. Jazz lovers should hit the riverside Jazz Dock *(jazzdock.cz)*, where a variety of world-class jazz is played nightly. For a more eclectic experience, try Palác Akropolis *(p132)*. This is the heart of the indie and world-music scene and has hosted the likes of the Pixies, Apollo 440 and Transglobal Underground.

10 On the Water

The calm waters of the Vltava are the perfect way to see Prague by night. Prague Boats *(prague-boats.cz)* offers a range of tours – by electric boat – that are suitable for families. Alternatively, the river is the perfect place to spend an evening revelling, whether on a sunset cruise or party boat (the Bukanyr music boat is recommended; *bukanyr.cz*).

Looking over Staré Město and the Vltava at night

TOP 10 LIVE MUSIC CLUBS

Reduta jazz club

1. Reduta
Reduta *(p123)* is all about jazz performances – Bill Clinton even played sax here.

2. U Malého Glena
This intimate club *(p102)* pairs world-class music with a relaxed vibe.

3. Ungelt
📍 M3 🏠 Jilská 1a
Head underground to enjoy jazz and blues with occasional funk and fusion.

4. AghaRTA
Local and international acts perform at this medieval Gothic cellar *(p93)*.

5. Jazz Republic
This family-owned venue offers great food and nightly performances by incredible jazz musicians *(p93)*.

6. Lucerna Music Bar
Lucerna's 80s and 90s weekend nights keep pumping out the retro classics *(p123)*.

7. Jilská 22
📍 L4 🏠 Jilská 22
It's all about EDM at this hip venue that specializes in dance music.

8. Futurum Music Bar
📍 D6 🏠 Zborovská 82/7
This spacious venue hosts acts from almost any genre you can think of.

9. Klub FAMU
📍 E4 🏠 Smetanovo nábř. 2
Find your new favourite local artist at this basement venue.

10. U Staré paní
📍 L5 🏠 Michalská 441/9
Enjoy classy cocktails and smooth jazz at this throwback cocktail bar.

PRAGUE DISHES

Nakládaný hermelín, a firm favourite in pubs

1 Nakládaný hermelín
Creamy with an edible rind, this soft cheese is marinated in oil with some pepper, garlic and spices. The main component of this is *hermelín*, the Czech Camembert. A popular bar snack, this is best enjoyed with dark Czech bread and a cold beer.

2 Knedlíky
These doughy dumplings are the side dish of choice for many gravy-laden Czech dishes. In addition to the savoury varieties, made with bread, potato or bacon *(špekové)*, *knedlíky* also come stuffed with fruit *(ovocné knedlíky)*, the most popular variety being plums *(švestkové)*.

3 Guláš
Not as spicy as its Hungarian cousin, Czech goulash is a rich beef stew minus the vegetables. It's always served with *knedlíky* (dumplings), usually made from a mix of bread and potato. Beef forms part of the standard recipe for this staple dish, but you can sometimes find goulash using venison, pork and even vegetarian variants.

4 Řízek
The traditional Czech take on schnitzel is a flattened pork cutlet, covered in flour, egg and breadcrumbs, then fried and served with potato salad. Many pubs offer a chicken or veal alternative, with chips on the side.

5 Utopence
These pickled sausages, slightly sour, fatty and always piled high with pickled onions, are an ideal accompaniment to the local beer, as a lunchtime or early evening snack.

6 Smažený sýr
Like fried mozzarella sticks, this battered block of deep-fried mild cheese is usually served with French fries *(hranolky)* and a tartar sauce. As with much of Czech cuisine, try not to think about the cholesterol.

7 Halušky
The Germans call these plump little noodles *spaetzle*. They are included in the Czech culinary canon as a nod to nearby Slovakia, from where they originate. You can order them *s zelím* (with sauerkraut) or *s bryndzou* (with a creamy, sharp cheese). The dish is a filling and pocket-friendly alternative to pasta.

Slovakian Halušky with cabbage and bacon

Svíčková na smetaně,
a Czech meat dish

8 Svíčková na smetaně

This is goulash's sweet cousin: slices of pot-roasted beef tenderloin are served in a carrot-sweetened cream sauce, topped with a dollop of whipped cream and cranberries. Apparently, this was one of President Václav Havel's favourite dishes. Like goulash, it's unthinkable to eat it without the *knedlíky* to mop up the sauce.

9 Vepřoknedlozelo

Vepřové, knedlíky a zelí – pork, dumplings and sauerkraut – are heavy on fat but big on flavour like true Czech soul food. Order it instead of goulash and impress your waiter with how acclimatized you are, assuming you pronounce it right, of course.

10 Rohlíky

The workhorse of the Prague diet, these ubiquitous banana-shaped bread rolls are served up to accompany the main meal at breakfast, lunch and dinner. Dip them in soft cheese or your dish's sauce, spread them with pâté or order them with a hot dog on nearly every street corner.

TOP 10
CZECH BEERS

1. Staropramen
The hometown favourite has a light, fruity flavour. Brewed in the Smíchov district, its popularity owes as much to marketing as it does to local pride.

2. Pilsner Urquell
The best-known Czech beer on the international market comes from the town of Plzeň, 80 km (50 miles) south-west of Prague. It has a hoppy flavour.

3. Krušovice
Rudolf II established the Krušovice brewery, which produces this sweet and somewhat flat beer. Try the syrupy dark *(tmavé)* variety.

4. Budvar
Brewed in the town of České Budějovice, the beer is no relation to the American Budweiser.

5. Velkopopovický Kozel
This strong, smooth beer is well worth seeking out – some consider it the world's finest.

6. Bakalář
Countryside lager brewed in Rakovník, 50 km (30 miles) west of Prague.

7. Gambrinus
Brewed by Pilsner Urquell, this is the best-selling beer in the country.

8. Bernard
This unpasteurized beer has a distinct, bittersweet flavour.

9. Únětické
This popular microbrew from a small family-run brewery can be hard to find but worth the effort.

10. Svijany
The brewery produces dark and light beers, including Svijanský Máz lager.

Staropramen beer

Patrons enjoying their drinks in U Fleků

BARS AND KAVÁRNAS

1 U Fleků

The city's oldest brewing pub, dating to 1499, U Fleků *(p124)* is famous for its delicious dark lager and somewhat more than modest prices. Despite what anyone might tell you, the Becherovka shots are not complimentary and the rounds will keep coming until you say *"ne"* five times. Very popular with tourists, and not without reason.

2 Café Slavia

Across from the National Theatre and on a busy river thoroughfare, Café Slavia *(p94)* with its 1930s Art Deco interior is a famous literary café. Theatregoers, actors and playwrights frequent this café. Enjoy a coffee and dessert at the end of the day or after a night at the theatre, admiring the view of the riverside, Charles Bridge and Prague Castle.

3 U Zlatého tygra

This legendary pub *(p94)*, famed as the haunt of the late writer Bohumíl Hrabal *(p57)*, serves the finest mug of Pilsner Urquell in Prague. Apart from the Pilsner beer, the brief menu features the famous beer cheese, snacks and coffee. Regulars were indifferent when Václav Havel brought Bill Clinton in for a cold glass when they were both serving presidents, so don't expect them to take much interest in you.

4 Café Savoy

With its Art Nouveau interiors and Neo-Renaissance style high ceiling, Café Savoy *(p103)* is considered one of the most gorgeous and stylish cafés in Prague. Set near the Kampa park and Petřín Hill, just a few steps from the Vltava river, this café provides the perfect setting to enjoy breakfast or lunch in a grand style. The regularly changing seasonal menu includes a variety of salads, roast meats and Czech specialities. Enjoy your coffee with one of their classic Czech desserts.

5 Kenton's

This is one of Prague's best cocktail bars. It may look like a Jazz Age time capsule, but Kenton's *(p93)* is actually a relative newcomer, and highly welcome at that. You'll find no bottle juggling, just serious mixology, very dry martinis and, if you're lucky, a seat. It remains open until 3am. You can also learn a few bartender's tricks at the regular mixology classes.

6 U Tří Růží

This good Czech restaurant and microbrewery *(p94)* feels just right for the middle of Staré Město. The decor includes several murals depicting the history of brewing in Czech lands. Beers brewed on the premises include a standard light, a dark lager, a Vienna red – from caramelized malt – and a wheat beer. The downstairs area can be crowded and noisy. Reservations are advised.

7 Grand Café Orient

Located on the first floor of the famous House of the Black Madonna, this café *(p94)* was designed during the Cubist movement in 1912 by Josef Gočár. Patrons will love the building's architecture and be fascinated by the tower of cakes that greets them at the entrance. Grand Café Orient serves tea, breakfast and lunch menus, as well as wine and cocktails.

8 Hemingway Bar

This is an old-fashioned cocktail bar *(p93)* exactly as it should be, with formally dressed barmen polishing up the glassware before they pour you the perfect Old Fashioned or Whiskey Sour. The cocktail menu has hundreds of classic mixes, and even a small selection of premium Czech, French and Swiss absinthe. Book ahead or you're likely to be turned away.

9 Black Angel's

This bar *(p93)*, located in the second basement of hotel U Prince, features 1930s-style decor among original Gothic and Romanesque stonemasonry. Sip on the excellent cocktails in the sophisticated interior, while enjoying fabulous views of the Old Town Square and city centre.

10 Pivovarský dům

Excellent, rustic Czech fare. The house brewmaster is always concocting new flavours for his drinks, such as coffee lager or champagne ale. This is a good place *(p124)* to visit if you prefer herbal or fruity flavoured beers such as cherry, nettle and coffee. You can also see the fermenting vats making beer, if the process of brewing interests you.

The dining room at the popular Pivovarský dům

SHOPS AND MARKETS

1 Botanicus

Here *(p92)* you'll find oils and salts for that hot bath your travel-weary feet crave, as well as perfumes, candles, soaps and every natural health and beauty product you can imagine. There are two branches right next to each other just off the Old Town Square.

2 Hračky U zlatého lva

This centrally located, multistorey toyshop *(p92)* stocks a huge selection of traditional Czech wooden toys, most of them locally produced. There's a Krtek (Little Mole – the most popular Czech cartoon character) theme through-out which will please travelling tots in search of souvenirs.

3 Art Deco

Enter this shop *(p92)* filled with antique furnishings, vintage clothing and one-of-a-kind knick-knacks and you'll feel you've stepped back into the First Republic. Kit yourself out in Jazz Age style, right down to the spats and cigarette holder, or dress up your parlour with an Art Nouveau clock or cordial set.

4 Erpet Bohemia Crystal

Set in the famous Old Town Square, this is a one-stop shop for glass and jewellery. Erpet *(p92)* sells Bohemian lead crystal, garnet jewellery, enamel glass and chandeliers,

Glass decanters at Erpet Bohemia Crystal

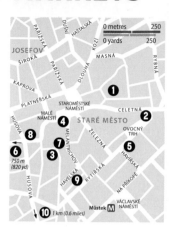

as well as fine goods from the Moser, Goebel and Swarovski manufacturers. Shoppers can ponder the purchases they're about to make over coffee in the shop's comfortable lounge area.

5 Dorotheum

⬚ M4 ⬚ Ovocný trh 2

Dorotheum offices throughout the world trace their roots back to the Vienna pawnbroking office, established by Emperor Josef I in 1707. As a registered member of the Association of International Auctioneers, Dorotheum holds large auctions several times a year and maintains a huge sales gallery of paintings and works of art, jewellery, silverware, glassware, fine china and furniture, as well as other collectors' items. Their regular auctions are popular with local as well as foreign clients.

6 Artěl

Named after a group of Bohemian artisans established in the early 1900s, Artěl *(p101)* has taken the time-honoured art of glassmaking and, working hand in hand with highly

Exquisite and colourful cut glass items at Artěl

8 Local Artists Praha
📍 L4 📌 Karlova 21

While walking through the "souvenir" Karlova street, set aside the time to stop at this small shop, where every item on display is a testimony to Czech traditional arts and crafts. The unique collection includes handmade pottery and beer cosmetics.

9 Havelské Tržiště
📍 M5 🕐 7am–7pm daily

The only preserved marketplace in the Staré Město dating back to 1232. In addition to Havelská street, where the current market is located, the original one extended to Rytířská street and Uhelný trh square, which run parallel to it. It offers a selection of fresh fruits and vegetables.

skilled craftspeople, has created a collection of fresh, whimsical yet elegant designs. It has created custom designs for several top luxury brands including Burberry and Gucci.

7 Manufaktura
This popular gift shop chain *(p92)*, an original Czech brand, is known for offering a unique range of natural cosmetic products and accessories as well as selling traditional Czech and Moravian souvenirs. Manufaktura's line of cosmetics and attractive accessories, including scented candles, porcelain and massage tools, are ideal for a home spa.

10 Náplavka Farmers' Market
📍 E6 📌 Náplavka 🕐 8am–3pm Sat
🌐 farmarshetrziste.cz

This riverfront food market is the place to be on summer Saturdays when the whole city seems to turn out to buy fresh produce, breads and meats. Even if you're not shopping, the atmosphere is infectious. Stroll the embankment and have a beer or coffee. Follow the Vltava south beyond the National Theatre to find the market.

Náplavka Farmers' Market on the Vltava riverbank

PRAGUE FOR FREE

1 Astronomical Clock
L4 **Old Town Hall**

Standing below the Gothic Old Town Hall, along with hundreds of fellow visitors, marvelling at the medieval clock as it goes through its hourly procession (on the hour from 9am to 11pm) is a rite of passage. It is rather brief and admittedly underwhelming, but a must-see.

2 Prague Castle Grounds
C2 **Prague Castle**
hrad.cz

Visiting the permanent collections at Prague Castle can cost a king's ransom in entry fees. What many visitors don't realize is that it is totally free to enter the castle grounds and wander around to your heart's content. Don't miss the changing of the castle guard on the hour from 7am to 8pm (7am to 6pm in winter).

3 Old Jewish Cemetery
Spread across seven sites in Prague, the Jewish Museum is world class, with impressive exhibits and admission fees priced to match. If paying the full fee is beyond your

The grave of Antonín Dvořák

budget, you can catch a small but worthwhile glimpse of the multitude of sombre tombstones in the Old Jewish Cemetery (p113) for free through a small window set in the western wall of the cemetery on Ulice 17. listopadu.

4 John Lennon Wall
This towering stretch of wall is covered with graffiti dedicated to Beatles frontman John Lennon. It is a relaxing – even spiritual – spot (p97). Occasionally, buskers belt out their own renditions of "Yesterday" or "Imagine". Peaceful Kampa Island (p98), a minute's walk to the east of the wall, is filled with hidden delights and well worth a wander.

5 Vyšehrad Cemetery
B6 **Vyšehrad**
praha-vysehrad.cz

The cemetery at Vyšehrad fortress (p127) is the country's most prominent burial ground and is free to enter. Fans of classical music will enjoy looking for the graves of Antonín Dvořák and Bedřich Smetana, among others. Many of the tombstones are works of art in their own right.

6 Botanical Garden of Charles University
F7 **Na Slupi 16** **10am–6pm daily; Apr–Aug: 10am–7:30pm daily** **bz-uk.cz**

A cosy green area in the centre of Prague, this garden opened in 1898 and gradually expanded to include an arboretum, greenhouses, ponds and a large alpine garden. It makes a pleasant place to relax.

7 Free Walking Tours
P4 **Staré Město**
extravaganzafreetour.com

This is a great way to explore Prague with a guide. Free Prague Tours is run by licensed English-speaking guides who are also history buffs.

Prague's Vltava river, as seen from Letná

Even with a generous tip at the end, you'll still save money. Tours normally begin at the Powder Gate at 11am and at Charles Bridge at 1pm.

8 View from Letná
E1 Greater Prague

Climb the steps at the northern end of Čechův most ("bridge" in Czech), north of Old Town Square for picture-postcard views of the Staré Město and the bridges traversing the river below. Keep an eye out for the metronome (p128) on the hill.

9 Wallenstein Garden
D2 Malá Strana
Apr–Oct: 7:30am–6pm Mon–Fri, 10am–6pm Sat & Sun; Jun–Sep: 7:30am–7pm Mon–Fri, 10am–7pm Sat & Sun senat.cz

Malá Strana is full of Renaissance and Baroque gardens that levy a fee to enter but this lovely 17th-century garden (p66) is free to the public. The palace (p100), home to the Czech Senate, can also be visited.

10 Vojanovy sady
D2 U lužického semináře 17

Malá Strana has many green pockets, but Vojan's gardens top them all for their romantic charm. Tulip beds, flowering fruit trees and the occasional peacock add to the fairy-tale atmosphere.

TOP 10
BUDGET TIPS

1. Opera and classical music in Prague is subsidized and tickets seldom cost more than a few thousand crowns.

2. Consider renting a private single or double hostel room. Many hostels offer these at a fraction of the price they would cost in a hotel.

3. Time your stay to avoid the peak seasons around holidays, when hotel rates go through the roof.

4. Consider renting an apartment if you're staying for three days or longer. You'll not only save money but will have more privacy.

5. Buy a discounted one-day or three-day pass for Prague's public transport. These are valid for the metro, trams, buses, trains and boats. You'll save money and not have to purchase tickets for each journey.

6. When arriving by plane, take the municipal bus into town from the airport. A single Kč40 ticket can often get you very close to your hotel.

7. Resist the temptation to hop into a taxi. Most distances in the city are easily walkable, and public transport is reliable and cheap.

8. Eat out at lunchtime instead of dinner to take advantage of the popular three-course set menus.

9. Skip wine at meals in favour of beer. Czech wines can vary greatly in quality; the local beer is generally cheaper and excellent quality.

10. Seek out pubs in outlying districts like Žižkov, where a half-litre (pint) mug of beer can cost half the price it does in the centre.

A classical music performance

FESTIVALS

1 Masopust
Shrove Tue

Locals dress up in masks, and sing and dance down the streets during this Czech carnival. Masopust translates to "meat-feasts" in Old Czech, alluding to the plethora of foodie feasts on offer as well. Celebrations are concentrated in the neighbourhood of Žižkov (p128).

2 May Day
1 May

It is customary for couples to visit the statue of the Czech Romantic poet Karel Hynek Mácha on Petřín Hill (p46). For others the national holiday is spent trying to forget the old obligatory Communist rallies.

3 Prague Spring International Music Festival
May–Jun

Bedřich Smetana's *Má vlast*, or *My Homeland* (p57), kicks off the annual three-week festival that draws classical music performers and fans from around the globe. The round of concerts closes with Beethoven's Ninth Symphony.

4 Tanec Praha
May, Jun

This international dance festival has become an annual part of Prague's festivities. The local dance scene has greatly benefited from it, and audiences can now see contemporary productions all year round.

5 Karlovy Vary International Film Festival
Jul

Hobnob with the stars while you attend screenings at this festival. Hundreds of partygoers turn the sleepy west Bohemian spa town, 130 km (81 miles) from Prague, upside down for nine days.

6 Street Theatre Festival
Jul

Za dveřmi (Behind the Door) is an international street art festival that presents drama, acrobatics, parades and juggling on the streets and squares of Prague.

7 Bohemia International Folklore Dance Festival
Aug

This festival has been a success since its first staging in 2005. It has now

Performers during the Masopust carnival

expanded beyond Prague, as DanceBohemia, and brings amateur folklore dance ensembles together from all around the world.

8 Prague Writer's Festival
Salman Rushdie, Susan Sontag and Elie Wiesel are just some of the internationally acclaimed authors who have attended this annual event, which takes place every spring.

9 Signal Festival
Oct
This annual festival of lights is one of the city's most popular events. Across four days, Prague is filled with magical artistic light displays that celebrate digital and creative culture.

10 Mikuláš, Vánoce, Silvestr
Dec
Christmas celebrations are largely devoid of religion, but the mulled wine starts flowing on St Nicholas's Day (6 December) and doesn't stop until the Christmas carp is all eaten and the New Year's Eve *(Silvestr)* fireworks arsenals are depleted.

Dancers at the Bohemia International Folklore Dance Festival

TOP 10
NATIONAL HOLIDAYS

1. Renewal of the Independent Czech State
1 Jan
Marks the 1993 split of Czechoslovakia.

2. Easter Monday
Mar–Apr
Custom dictates that men give women a gentle whipping with a branch. There are calls to end this tradition.

3. Labour Day
1 May
Romantics lay flowers before the statue of Karel Hynek Mácha on Petřín Hill.

4. Day of Liberation
8 May
Plaques around town are adorned with flowers to remember those killed by the Germans in 1945.

5. Cyril and Methodius Day
5 Jul
The Greek missionaries *(p118)* brought both Christianity and the Cyrillic alphabet to the Slavs.

6. Jan Hus Day
6 Jul
Czechs commemorate one of the greatest figures of Czech history *(p29)*.

7. Czech Statehood Day
28 Sep
Bohemia's history is recalled on St Wenceslas Day, as most Czechs call it.

8. Independence Day
28 Oct
In 1918, Czechoslovakia declared itself independent of Austro-Hungary.

9. Day of the Fight for Freedom and Democracy
17 Nov
The anniversary of the Velvet Revolution *(p11)* is marked with candles and flowers.

10. Christmas
24–26 Dec
Streets fill with carp sellers and revellers drinking mulled wine.

AREA BY AREA

Roofs of Staré Město

STARÉ MĚSTO

Prague's heart is a layered cake of history dating back several hundred years: the oldest of its buildings have double cellars, owing to a flood-prevention programme that buried the original streets 3 m (10 ft) beneath those that exist today. Architecturally, it embraces every epoch, from the Romanesque to the Brutalist style of the mid-1970s Kotva department store. Historically, the burghers of the Staré Město (Old Town) were ill at ease with the castle district, and vice versa, with the town being a bastion of Protestant feistiness. Staré Město is still livelier than Malá Strana and Hradčany, with cafés, clubs, restaurants and theatres that provide entertainment around the clock.

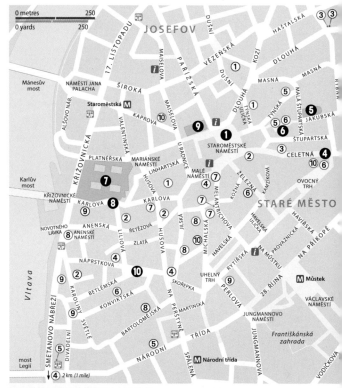

For places to stay in this area, see p144

Old Town Square lined with Gothic and Baroque façades

1 Old Town Square

Over the centuries, this now peaceful square (p28) at the heart of the city has witnessed hundreds of executions, political capitulations and, more recently, riotous ice-hockey cele-brations. Today, the action is more likely to come from the crowds of tourists and Praguers, enjoying a coffee or a glass of beer at a pavement café. Dominated by the Church of Our Lady before Týn (p51), the square is always buzzing; in winter and summer, it's a wonderful place to watch the world go by.

2 Municipal House

🗺 P3 🚇 Náměstí Republiky 5
🌐 obecnidum.cz 🔊🔌

National Revival artist Alfons Mucha was one of many to lend his talents to the Municipal House (Obecní dům), Prague's star Art Nouveau attraction. One of its most striking features is Karel Špillar's mosaic above the main entrance, entitled *Homage to Prague*. It also has a firm place in history as it was from the Municipal House that Czechoslovakia was declared an independent state in 1918. Today, it is home to restaurants, cafés, exhibition halls, shops and the Prague Symphony Orchestra at Smetana Hall (p72).

3 Powder Gate

🗺 P4 🚇 Náměstí Republiky
🕙 10am–7pm daily (Jul & Aug: to 9pm; Oct–Mar: to 6pm; Dec: to 8pm) 🔌

In the 15th century, King Vladislav II laid the cornerstone for this tower at the city's eastern gate, intended to comple-ment the Royal Court nearby. The name of this monument comes from its 17th-century role as a gunpowder store. The tower was damaged during Prussian attacks in 1757. The Neo-Gothic façade seen today, with its ornate sculptural decoration, dates from 1876.

Traditional house sign, Celetná

sanctuary. The church, founded in 1232 by Wenceslas I, is best known for the legend of the mummified arm (*p60*) hanging above the door. The church has excellent acoustics so make sure you don't miss the organ recitals held here.

6 Ungelt
🗺 M3

Also known as the Týn Courtyard, this was a fortified merchants' settlement in the 10th century. The Baroque and Renaissance houses were completely renovated in the early 1990s, creating what is now one of the Old Town's most charming mercantile centres.

4 Celetná
🗺 M4

The medieval route from the silver-mining town of Kutná Hora in Bohemia passed down the street known today as Celetná, through Old Town Square and on to Prague Castle.

5 Basilica of St James
🗺 N3 🏠 Malá Štupartská 6
🕐 9:30am–noon & 2–4pm daily (except Mon & during Mass)
🌐 prahaina.minorite.cz

The Gothic and Baroque interior wins the award for Prague's creepiest

7 Clementinum
🗺 K4 🏠 Křížovnická 190, Mariánské náměstí 5 & Karlova 1
📞 222 220879 🕐 Jan–Mar: 10am–6pm daily; Apr–Sep: 9am–8pm daily; Oct–Dec: 9am–7pm daily ♿

Built in the mid-17th century as a Jesuit college, the Clementinum now houses the National Library. Noted astronomer Johannes Kepler discovered the laws of planetary motion atop the Astronomical Tower. There is a beautiful Baroque library, and the Mirror Chapel hosts various concerts.

PRAGUE'S WALLS AND GATES

Prague's walls started going up in the 13th century, protecting the new settlement from the distant Tartars. The town was accessible via wall gates. As gradual developments in military technology made walls and moats less effective forms of defence, Praguers found new uses for their fortifications. The broad ramparts became parks, complete with benches, lamps and even cafés. The city kept the habit of locking its gates at night well into the 19th century, however.

8 Karlova
K4

You will inevitably get lost trying to follow Karlova street from the Old Town Square to Charles Bridge; relax and enjoy the bewildering, twisting alleys crammed with shops and cafés.

9 St Nicholas Cathedral
L3 Staroměstské náměstí 10am–5pm Mon–Sat, noon–5pm Sun svmikulas.cz

This Baroque jewel began as a parish church. During World War I, it was used as a garrison church for Czech soldiers. It now belongs to the Hussite Church and also operates as a concert hall.

10 Bethlehem Square
K5 Chapel: 9am–6pm daily bethlehem chapel.eu

The 15th-century Catholic reformer Jan Hus (p29) preached in the reconstructed chapel on the square's north side. The church was converted into apartments in the 18th century but was lovingly restored to its former state in the 1950s.

Clementinum's Baroque library, adorned with frescoes

A STROLL AROUND STARÉ MĚSTO

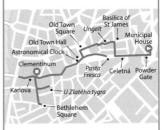

Morning

After breakfast at the **Municipal House** café (p89), take a guided tour of the building, then go and climb the **Powder Gate** (p89).

Wander down **Celetná**, ducking through the arcade to Štupartská and the **Basilica of St James**. If you have at least 45 minutes before the top of the hour, make your way through the **Ungelt** courtyard to the **Old Town Square** (p28). Join a tour of the **Old Town Hall** and get a backstage view of the Apostles' show on the **Astronomical Clock** (p82). Otherwise, spend some time shopping in the Ungelt, then join the crowd below the clock outside to see the spectacle. For lunch, head slightly out of the square to **Pasta Fresca** (p95).

Afternoon

Return to the Old Town Square, then enter the meandering turns of **Karlova** and wander past the area's old buildings before turning south to reach **Bethlehem Square**. Take a tour of the Bethlehem Chapel. If you'd like a break, have a beer at **U Zlatého tygra** (p94), a three-minute walk north, then retrace your steps to Karlova to visit the **Clementinum**.

After freshening up, take in a concert or a performance at the theatre. Curtains go up around 7:30pm, so dine afterwards.

Shoppers at Prague's famous Palladium mall

Shops

1. Amadea
L4 ⌂ Melantrichova 6
Find a wide range of wooden products such as ornaments, decorations, souvenirs, utensils and kitchenware, all hand-picked by the owners.

2. Moser
M4 ⌂ Staroměstské náměstí 15
Browse through classic crystal and cut-glass objects produced by this well-known manufacturer.

3. Palladium
P3 ⌂ Náměstí Republiky 1
One of the most popular shopping destinations in downtown Prague, Palladium has 200 shops offering exciting shopping and dining experiences to visitors.

4. Erpet Bohemia Crystal
L4 ⌂ Staroměstské náměstí 27
Located across from the Astronomical Clock, this megastore has an exclusive collection of Bohemian crystal, art glass, fine costume jewellery, crystal figurines and much more. The staff are friendly and attentive.

5. Material
M3 ⌂ Týn 1, Ungelt
Czech tradition in designer crystal and glassware gets a modern makeover at this shop in the Ungelt courtyard. Admire the eye-catching stemware, vases, dishes and candle-holders, all presented in a space that fuses classical and modern design.

6. Botanicus
M3 ⌂ Týn 2 & 3
The store's all-natural health and beauty products are produced at a "historic village" east of Prague; enquire about tours. Herbs, oils and other seasonings are also sold here.

7. Manufaktura
L4 ⌂ Melantrichova 17
This is a one-stop shop for all your small souvenir needs, including Czech folk crafts and traditional wooden toys. In addition to these items, there are also naturally made cosmetics and toiletries featuring an odd assortment of ingredients, such as Czech beer, wine and thermal salt.

8. Art Deco
L4 ⌂ Michalská 21
Come here for a range of goods including handbags, jewellery, ceramics, glassware and vintage clothing inspired by the early 20th century.

9. Český Porcelán
M5 ⌂ Perlová 1
Bohemian porcelain might not be as prestigious as Bohemian crystal, but it makes a pretty souvenir or present.

10. Hračky U zlatého lva
N4 ⌂ Celetná 32
Explore the range of traditional wooden toys and other board games here (p80).

Nightclubs

1. Kenton's
🄵 L2 🄰 V Kolkovně 3 🅆 kentons.cz
One of Prague's fancier bars, Kenton's has a classy vibe with an elegant interior and a wooded counter. There's a good range of interesting cocktails.

2. Hemingway Bar
🄵 J5 🄰 Karolíny Světlé 26
🅆 hemingwaybar.cz
Inspired by Ernest Hemingway, the great author and one of the most well-known bar lovers, this place offers his favourite liquors such as Absinthe, a variety of rum, champagne, and excels in mixology.

3. Roxy
🄵 N2 🄰 Dlouhá 33 🅆 roxy.cz
In addition to the best dance parties in town, this club hosts experimental theatre and live bands.

4. Jazz Republic
🄵 M6 🄰 Jilská 1a 🅆 jazzrepublic.cz
One of Prague's top music clubs, Jazz Republic features live jazz, funk, blues, dance, Latin, fusion or world music seven nights a week.

5. Vagon
🄵 L6 🄰 Národní třída 25 🅆 vagon.cz
One of the originals for exciting live music, this place hosts blues or rock bands most nights, with a mix of well-known and emerging talents.

A band performing at the popular nightclub, Roxy

Classic bar with shelves of drinks at Black Angel's Bar

6. AghaRTA Jazz Centrum
🄵 M4 🄰 Železná 16 🅆 agharta.cz
Named after Miles Davis's seminal album from the 1970s, this club has daily performances by top Czech musicians and hosts the annual AghaRTA Prague Jazz Festival.

7. Black Angel's
🄵 L4 🄰 Staroměstské náměstí 29
🅆 blachangelsbar.com
Designed in the style of a Prohibition era speakeasy, this attractive bar offers creative drinks and cocktails.

8. Friends
🄵 K6 🄰 Bartolomějshá 11
🅆 friendsclub.cz
Prague's best gay cocktail bar has a steady following among expats and locals. Evenings are filled with a rich mix of DJ sets, karaoke and themed parties or quizzes.

9. Zlatý Strom
🄵 K4 🄰 Karlova 6 🅆 zlatystrom.com
Enjoy unusual views of the Prague night sky through the glass ceilings of this subterranean club. There are two dance floors inside.

10. Caffrey's
🄵 M3 🄰 Staroměstské náměstí 10
🅆 caffreys.cz
This lively Irish bar is one of the most popular in town. The beer terrace in front of the pub offers the perfect setting to enjoy drinks during summer.

Cafés and Pubs

1. Café Obecní dům
P3 🏠 Náměstí Republiky 5
🌐 havarnaod.cz
Stop for breakfast at this café with Art Nouveau interiors, before setting off for a day exploring Staré Město.

2. U Tří Růží
L5 🏠 Husova 10 🌐 u3r.cz
This charming 15th-century brewery and restaurant, on Husova street, serves on-site brewed beers and a menu of Czech classics.

3. Lokál Dlouháááá
N2 🏠 Dlouhá 33 🌐 lokal-dlouha. ambi.cz
Rumoured to serve the city's freshest Pilsner Urquell beer, delivered to the door in big tanks.

4. Terasa U Prince
L4 🏠 Staroměstské náměstí 29
🌐 terasauprince.com
Visit this café and restaurant on the rooftop terrace of Hotel U Prince for a truly memorable dining experience.

5. Café Slavia
J6 🏠 Národní třída 1 🌐 cafeslavia.cz
Set in the historical centre of Prague, this café offers Czech and international cuisine that include salads, fish and meat specialities.

6. Grand Café Orient
N4 🏠 Ovocný trh 19
🌐 grandcafeorient.cz
With its Cubist style decor, the specialities at this elegant café include the traditional Czech pastry, *kubistický věneček*.

7. U Zlatého tygra
L4 🏠 Husova 17 🌐 uzlatehotygra.cz
Located in the heart of Staré Město, this pub is renowned for its old world charm and Pilsner beer.

8. Prague Beer Museum
J5 🏠 Smetanovo nábřeží 22
🌐 praguebeermuseum.cz
This is one of the four branches of this popular pub with around 30 Czech beers on tap.

9. Atmosphere
J5 🏠 Smetanovo náb. 14
🌐 atmosha.cz
This café, pub and restaurant offers its customers tank beer, Italian and Czech wines, plus various Czech dishes.

10. Café Ebel
L3 🏠 Kaprova 11 🌐 ebelcoffee.com
You won't find a better cup of coffee in the city than at Ebel, which uses beans from all over the world. It is not far away from the Old Town Square *(p28)*.

Diners on the rooftop terrace of Terasa U Prince

Restaurants

1. Maitrea

ⓠ M3 ⓐ Týnská ulička 6
ⓦ restaurace-maitrea.cz · ⓚⓚ

Located just off the Old Town Square, Maitrea is an excellent vegetarian and vegan restaurant, which serves traditional Czech fare alongside Mexican, Thai and other international dishes.

2. Wine O'Clock

ⓠ K4 ⓐ Liliová 16 ⓒ Sun & Mon
ⓦ wineoclockprague.com · ⓚⓚ

Enjoy tasty Italian small plates, from bruschetta pomodoro to aubergine parmiggiana, with a glass of wine at this cozy establishment.

3. Pasta Fresca

ⓠ M4 ⓐ Celetná 11 ⓦ pasta-fresca.net · ⓚⓚⓚ

Chef Tomáš Mykytyn makes regional Italian dishes with seasonal ingredients. Sommeliers are on hand to guide diners through the wine menu.

4. V Zátiší

ⓠ K5 ⓐ Liliová 1 ⓦ vzatisi.cz · ⓚⓚⓚ

Sample modern and unconventional versions of traditional Czech and international dishes at this well-established fine dining restaurant.

5. Divinis

ⓠ M3 ⓐ Týnská 21 ⓒ Sun
ⓦ divinis.cz · ⓚⓚⓚ

This high-end wine bar and restaurant manages to balance a modern feel with a traditional Italian atmosphere. Good-quality wines complement the classic Sicilian specialities.

Interior of Maitrea, a popular restaurant

6. Sad Man's Tongue

ⓠ K6 ⓐ Konvihtshá 7 ⓦ sadmanstongue.com · ⓚⓚ

This popular bar and bistro serves up a big helping of Americana in the heart of Prague.

7. Bistro Monk

ⓠ L4 ⓐ Michalshá 20
ⓦ bistromonh.cz · ⓚⓚ

Prepared from local produce, the food at Bistro Monk is simple and delicious. Try the pancakes with blueberry sauce.

8. Hosarowa

ⓠ L5 ⓐ Jilshá 6 ⓦ hosarowa.business.site · ⓚⓚ

Come here for Prague's best Korean barbecue, along with other classics like bibimbap and garak-guksu.

9. Století

ⓠ N2 ⓐ Karolíny Světlé 21
ⓦ stoleti.cz · ⓚⓚ

Try dishes named after Czech artists, writers and singers in a simple but stylish dining room. The menu has a good list of vegetarian options.

10. Plzeňská restaurace Obecní dům

ⓠ P3 ⓐ Náměstí Republiky 5
ⓦ pivniceod.cz · ⓚⓚ

Classic Czech food is served in a lively setting here. The extensive à la carte menu features dishes such as roast duck and grilled ribs.

MALÁ STRANA

Founded in 1257, Malá Strana (the Little Quarter) is built on the slopes below the castle hill with magnificent views across the river to Malá Strana. Floods, fires and war kept construction going on the Vltava's left bank; very few of the original Romanesque and Gothic buildings remain. During the reign of the Habsburgs, grand palaces were built in Baroque style, and today many of these serve as parliament or government buildings and embassies. The area is filled with quaint churches and dominated by beautiful Baroque buildings that flank the winding streets, which rise steeply away from the river and lead to splendid views of Petřín Park. In between the streets are small squares adorned with some of the city's grandest structures and home to the best dining options in Prague.

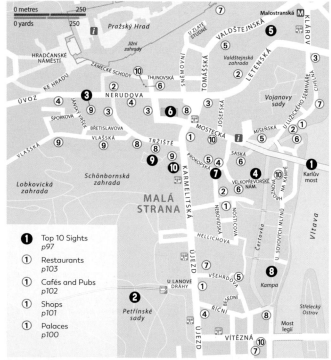

❶	Top 10 Sights p97
①	Restaurants p103
①	Cafés and Pubs p102
①	Shops p101
①	Palaces p100

For places to stay in this area, see p145

The iconic Charles Bridge over the Vltava river

1 Charles Bridge

For almost all visitors to Prague, this spectacular Gothic bridge (p32), crossing the Vltava from the castle complex to the Staré Město, remains their most memorable image of the city long after they have returned home.

2 Petřín Hill

A more than welcome respite from the maze of tiny, generally crowded streets in the city below is this sprawling park looking down over spires and rooftops. Enjoy the views all the way up the hill by taking the funicular (p47).

3 Nerudova

C2

A picturesque narrow street lined with former palaces, Nerudova leads uphill from Malostranské náměstí's winding side streets to Prague Castle (p22). It is named after 19th-century Czech writer and poet Jan Neruda (1834–91) who lived in the House of the Two Suns. Traditionally an artists' quarter, the street is worth exploring for its many craft shops and galleries. It is also home to one of the most concentrated collections of historic house signs (p58) in the city.

4 John Lennon Wall

D3 **Velkopřevorské náměstí**

Prague's street artists and the secret police once waged a long running paint battle here, as the latter constantly tried to eradicate the graffiti artists' work (p82). The original artwork, created by students after Lennon's assassination, has been painted over many times, but the John Lennon Peace Club still gathers annually at this self-made shrine to sing the former Beatle's praises – and his songs.

5 Wallenstein Garden

D2 **Apr–Oct: 7am–7pm daily**

Laid out in the grounds of the Baroque Wallenstein Palace (p118) these gardens have not changed since they were created by Duke Albrecht of Wallenstein in the 17th century. The garden's most notable features include a series of magnificent bronze statues and a loggia decorated with scenes from the Trojan War.

A bronze sculpture at Wallenstein Garden

6 St Nicholas Church
🗺 C2 🏛 Malostranské náměstí
🕐 Hours vary, chech website
🌐 stnicholas.cz 🔗

In the early 18th century, Jesuits constructed this stunning example of Baroque architecture on the site of a former Gothic parish. This prominent Prague landmark was designed by the acclaimed father and son Baroque architects, Christoph and Kilian Dientzenhofer, while other leading artists adorned the interior with exquisite carvings, statues and frescoes. From the 1950s the clock tower often served as an observation and spying point for the state security. For an extra fee, you can climb the tower for a memorable view over the orange rooftops of Malá Strana.

7 Maltézské náměstí
🗺 C3

The Knights of Malta once had an autonomous settlement here, and the square still bears their name. Search for the Bench of Václav Havel in the centre of the square. Hiding just a few steps from the square to the east is the 12th-century Church of Our Lady below the Chain, whose name refers to the chain used in the Middle Ages to close the monastery gatehouse.

8 Kampa Island
🗺 D3–4

The tiny Čertovka (Devil's Canal) that separates Kampa from Malá Strana was once the town's "laundry", milling area and, in the 17th century, home to a thriving pottery industry. A popular park now covers the island's southern end, while the northern half is home to elegant embassies, restaurants and hotels.

**Formal flower beds
of the Vrtba Garden**

9 Vrtba Garden

📍 C3 🏠 Karmelitshá 25
📅 Apr–Oct: 10am–6pm daily
🌐 vrtbovsha.cz

Enjoy magnificent views of Prague Castle and the Malá Strana from the highest point of this beautiful Baroque garden laid out by architect František Maximilián Kaňka in about 1720.

10 Church of Our Lady Victorious

📍 C3 🏠 Karmelitshá 9 📅 Church: 8:30am–6pm Mon–Sat, 8:30am–7pm Sun; Museum of the Infant Jesus of Prague: 9:30am–5pm Mon–Sat, 1–6pm Sun

Also known as the Church of the Infant Jesus of Prague, Prague's first Baroque church (1611) got its name and its Catholic outlook after the Battle of White Mountain (p9). Visitors flock to see the church's miracle-working statue of the infant Christ (p50).

**Lavish Baroque interior of
St Nicholas Church**

A DAY IN MALÁ STRANA

Morning

You can approach the Little Quarter from Staré Město as royal processions once did, by crossing **Charles Bridge** (p32), or you can save your energy for the day ahead, and start from the top of the hill and walk down. Get to **Nerudova** (p97) from one of the many side streets leading from Hradčany and stroll down, window shopping at the many craft outlets on your way. As long as you go downhill, you'll end up at the area's central hub, **Malostranské náměstí**. Here, spend at least an hour admiring **St Nicholas Church**. Pause for lunch at a café on Malostranské náměstí.

Afternoon

After lunch, take Tomášská to the **Wallenstein Garden** (p66). Tiptoe through the tulips at **Vojanovy sady** (p83) and continue down U lužického semináře under Charles Bridge and onto the lovely **Kampa Island**. Explore the island, then head off to check the writing on the **John Lennon Wall** (p82) before visiting the **Church of Our Lady Victorious** and finally enjoy the magnificent evening views from the highest point of **Vrtba Garden**.

In the evening, relax at the Bench of Václav Havel in the middle of Maltézské náměstí, or head to **U Malého Glena** (p102) to relax while listening to jazz and blues.

Palaces

1. Nostitz Palace
⬚ D3 ⬚ Maltézské náměstí 1
Take in the restoration work at this 17th-century palace while enjoying a chamber music concert. The palace now serves as the seat of the Czech Ministry of Culture.

2. Thun-Hohenstein Palace
⬚ C2 ⬚ Nerudova 20
The Kolowrat family's heraldic eagles support the portal of this palace. Built by Giovanni Santini-Aichel in 1721, the building is now home to the Italian Embassy.

3. Liechtenstein Palace
⬚ C2 ⬚ Malostranské náměstí 13 ⬚ amu.cz
Originally several different houses, the Liechtenstein Palace fused in the 16th century. Today, it is home to Prague's Academy of Music and hosts concerts and recitals.

4. Morzin Palace
⬚ C2 ⬚ Nerudova 5
The two giant Moors (hence Morzin) bearing up the Romanian Embassy's façade are said to wander about Malá Strana streets at night.

5. Wallenstein Palace
⬚ D2 ⬚ Valdštejnské náměstí 4 ⬚ 10am–6pm Sat ⬚ senat.cz ⬚
General Wallenstein pulled out all the stops creating what is essentially a monument to himself. On the palace's frescoes, the Thirty Years' War commander had himself depicted as both Achilles and Mars.

6. Buquoy Palace
⬚ D3 ⬚ Velkopřevorské náměstí 2
This pink stucco palace and the John Lennon Wall are separated by only a few steps, but they are miles apart aesthetically. The French Ambassador helped preserve the graffiti.

7. Michna Palace
⬚ C4 ⬚ Újezd 40
Francesco Caratti modelled this palace on Versailles in the 17th century. It is home to the Sokol Physical Culture Movement.

8. Schönborn Palace
⬚ C3 ⬚ Tržiště 15 ⬚ schoenbrunn.at
Count Colloredo-Mansfeld owned the palace in the 17th century: having lost a leg in the Thirty Years' War, he had the stairs rebuilt so he could ride his horse into the building.

9. Lobkowicz Palace (Převorovských)
⬚ B3 ⬚ Vlašská 19 ⬚ lobkowicz.cz
Home to the German Embassy. In 1989 hundreds of East Germans found their way to the West by scrambling over the back fence of this embassy building.

10. Kaunitz Palace
⬚ C3 ⬚ Mostecká 15
The Yugoslav (now Serbian) Embassy sat quietly in its pink and yellow stucco palace for more than 300 years until war made it a popular spot for protests.

The picture gallery at Nostitz Palace

Lovely entrance of Květinářstvi u Červéneho lva

Shops

1. Bel Art Gallery
📍 C3 🏠 Karmelitská 26
This small fine art gallery and shop, set in a 17th-century building, sells contemporary paintings, sculptures and ceramic works from more than 30 acclaimed artists. International shipping is available.

2. Shakespeare a Synové
📍 D3 🏠 U Lužického semináře 10
This bookstore specializes in foreign books and several titles in English, German and French. It offers a space for literary readings and discussions.

3. Muzeum Slivovice R. Jelínek
📍 D2 🏠 U Lužického semináře 48
🌐 muzeumslivovice.cz
Head to the shop of this distillery museum to pick up a bottle of *slivovice*, a traditional Czech plum spirit. Book a tasting to sample it before buying.

4. Curiomat
📍 B2 🏠 Nerudova 45
Just under New Castle Steps, this small shop sells original Czech puppets, gifts, toys, ceramics, jewellery, art and enamel tableware.

5. Artěl
📍 D3 🏠 U Lužického semináře 7
This store is known for exquisite mouth-blown and hand-engraved glassware and crystalware for decor of unique design motifs.

6. Květinářstvi u Červéneho lva
📍 D3 🏠 Saská
It appears as if a jungle is sprouting from the hole in the wall that is the Flowershop at the Red Lion. Spruce up your apartment or hotel room with their unique arrangements.

7. Perníkový panáček
📍 D2 🏠 Cihelna 2a
Located near the entrance to the Franz Kafka museum, this little side-street bakery has all manner of gingerbread creations, which make for great gifts.

8. Malostranské starožitnictví
📍 C2 🏠 Malostranské náměstí 28
This antiques store is a treasure trove of jewellery, watches, porcelain objects, silverware, coins and photographs. It also sells musical instruments.

9. Designum Gallery
📍 C2 🏠 Nerudova 27
This design boutique offers the works of up-and-coming artists apart from the established brands and designers. The highlights at the boutique include glass, porcelain as well as contemporary jewellery.

10. Orel and Friends
📍 C2 🏠 Nerudova 6
A wide selection of traditional Czech crafts, including ceramics, jewellery, handbags, leather-bound books and more, are available at this unique store.

Cafés and Pubs

Lovely Beatles-themed interior of the Wall Pub

1. Bakeshop Little Bakery
D2 **U Lužičého seminátí 22**
This little bakery serves pastries, breads, quiches and desserts. It also has a daily changing menu of fresh juices, smoothies and homemade soup served with croutons.

2. Café Kafičko
C3 **Maltézshé náměstí 15**
This café, with its excellent coffee and homemade cakes, proves to be the perfect getaway from the cold of the winter or the summer crowds.

3. Baráčnická rychta
C3 **Tržiště 23**
This wood-panelled beer hall, housed in a Modernist 1930s building, is a little piece of traditional Czech Republic in Malá Strana.

4. Cukrkávalimonáda
C3 **Lázeňshá 7**
Located opposite the entrance to the Church of Our Lady below the Chain, this popular little

patisserie is all about three things: *cukr* (sugar), *káva* (coffee) and *limonáda* (lemonade).

5. Alebrijes
D2 **U Lužického Semináře 109/38** **alebrijescocina mexicana.com/general-1**
Come to this cosy restaurant and bar for a relaxed meal with friends and family, and enjoy traditional Mexican drinks and cuisine.

6. U Kocoura
C2 **Nerudova 2**
You might think the regulars at this pub on Malá Strana's main drag would be used to tourists by now, but don't be surprised if every face turns to meet you. It serves excellent Pilsner.

7. Kofárna Café
D4 **Zborovshá 60**
In addition to excellent coffee, Kofárna offers many plant-based food options too. Try the famous Israeli hummus.

8. Café Bella Vida
D4 **Malostranské nábřezí 3**
This café serves its own coffee blend as well as delectable mini-desserts and sandwiches. Sit in the cosy garden and enjoy the beautiful views of Charles Bridge and Prague Castle.

9. U Malého Glena
C3 **Karmelitshá 23** **malyglen.cz**
Prague's smallest jazz venue, "At Small Glen's", also has a cosy restaurant where you can enjoy a variety of food and brunch at weekends.

10. The Wall Pub
D3 **Hroznová 495/6**
Less than a minute's walk from the John Lennon Wall, this pub is all about celebrating the legendary singer. Enjoy steaks and burgers in the garden.

Restaurants

1. Cantina
🅰 C4 🏠 Újezd 38 🆆 cantinana brezi.cz · Ⓚ Ⓚ

The fajitas here are great; choose from chicken, beef, pork or shrimp.

2. Augustine Restaurant
🅰 D2 🏠 Letenshá 12/33 🆆 augustine-restaurant.cz · Ⓚ Ⓚ Ⓚ

This restaurant serves European cuisine prepared with seasonal ingredients and a wide selection of drinks.

3. Malostranská Beseda
🅰 C2 🏠 Malostranské náměstí 21 ☎ 257 409112 · Ⓚ Ⓚ

Set in an elegant building in the heart of Little Quarter, this cosy place serves traditional Czech food and beer.

4. Czech Slovak Restaurant
🅰 C4 🏠 Újezd 20 🆆 czech slovah.cz · Ⓚ Ⓚ Ⓚ

This place brings traditional Czech and Slovak dishes into the 21st century in an artistic fashion.

5. Ichnusa Botega Bistro
🅰 D4 🏠 Plashá 5 ☎ 605 375012 · Ⓚ Ⓚ Ⓚ

A family-run bistro which offers a delicious range of Sardinian dishes.

6. Kampa Park
🅰 D3 🏠 Na Kampě 8b 🆆 hampapark.com · Ⓚ Ⓚ Ⓚ

This top riverside restaurant serves Continental classics and fusion cuisine.

PRICE CATEGORIES

For a three-course meal for one with half a bottle of wine (or equivalent meal), taxes and extra charges

Ⓚ under Kč500 Ⓚ Ⓚ Kč500–Kč1,000
Ⓚ Ⓚ Ⓚ over Kč1,000

---

7. Terasa U Zlaté studně
🅰 C2 🏠 U Zlaté studně 4 🆆 terasa uzlatestudne.cz · Ⓚ Ⓚ Ⓚ|

With its picturesque views, this fine dining restaurant offers the perfect setting to celebrate special occasions with friends and family.

8. Coda Restaurant
🅰 C3 🏠 Tržiště 9 🆆 coda restaurant.cz · Ⓚ Ⓚ Ⓚ

Enjoy the stunning views from the rooftop terrace of the Aria Hotel while sampling delicious Czech dishes.

9. St Martin
🅰 C3 🏠 Vlašshá 7 🆆 stmartin.cz · Ⓚ Ⓚ

Try traditional Czech dishes alongside Asian twists on American classics.

10. Café Savoy
🅰 C4 🏠 Vítězná 5 🆆 cafesavoy.ambi.cz · Ⓚ Ⓚ Ⓚ

This feels just like a Prague café should, with high ceilings and huge windows.

Patrons at the busy Café Savoy

PRAGUE CASTLE AND HRADČANY

Founded by Prince Bořivoj in the 9th century, Prague Castle and its attendant cathedral tower overlook the city from the long hill known as Hradčany. The surrounding town was founded in 1320, becoming home to servants' hovels and, after the cataclysmic fire of 1541, grand palaces. Renaissance and Baroque reconstructions in the area created much of what visitors see today. At the castle, primitive defences were removed, making room for gardens, parade grounds and the other needs of a modern empire. When the Habsburgs moved the imperial seat to Vienna, Hradčany seemed to become preserved in time. The area abounds with interesting sights for art and history lovers, as well as hidden lanes and parks – in short, a total expression of the Czech nation's shifting epochs and politics.

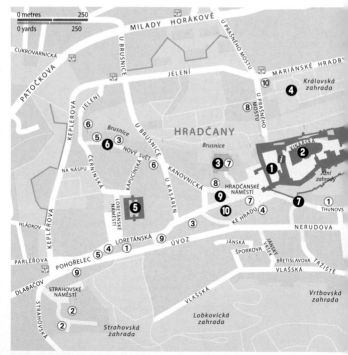

**A Bronzino painting at
the Sternberg Palace**

1 Prague Castle

The first and main focus of most tourists' visit to the city of Prague is the majestically located and architecturally varied castle complex (p22). Its determined survival in the face of an often turbulent history seems only to heighten the castle's lure for visitors. Despite its medieval appearance, it is still as much of a political stronghold as it has always been, and currently serves as the office of the country's president.

2 St Vitus Cathedral

The Gothic splendour of St Vitus's (p26) spires can be seen from almost every vantage point in the city, but don't miss the opportunity to see its beautiful stained-glass windows and imposing gargoyles up close.

3 Sternberg Palace

📍 B2 🏠 Hradčanské náměstí 15

This fine Baroque building, dating from 1698, houses the National Gallery's collection of European art from the classical to the Baroque. Spread over three floors, it is without doubt the country's best collection from the period. Its highlights include works by Rubens, Rembrandt and El Greco.

4 Royal Garden

📍 C1 🏠 U Prašného mostu
🕐 Apr–Oct: 10am–dusk daily
🌐 hrad.cz

This garden was originally laid out in 1534 by Ferdinand I. Although today's visitors may regret the disappearance of the maze and the pineapple trees that once featured here, they are likely to appreciate the absence of Rudolf II's freely roaming lions and tigers. In the English-style garden are the former presidential residence (the First Lady didn't like it), the *sgraffitoed* Ball Game Hall and Queen Anne's Summer Palace (Letohrádek královny Anny), also known as the Belvedere.

Beautiful ceiling frescoes in the Loreta

5 Loreta

The onion-domed white towers of this Baroque 17th-century church (*p34*) complex are like something out of a fairy tale.

6 Nový Svět
A2

Nestled below Loreta (*p34*), at the head of the Stag Moat, is Nový Svět (New World), the best street in town for a romantic stroll. The low houses were built in the 17th century to replace slums built for castle workers after their houses burned down in 1541. They have been spruced up, but are otherwise unspoiled. Rudolf II's choleric astronomer Tycho Brahe lived at No 1.

7 New Castle Steps
C2

The Royal Route, established in the 15th century for the coronation of George of Poděbrady, covered the distance from the Municipal House on Náměstí Republiky (*p89*) to the castle. The last stretch of steps climbed the hill here at the Zámecké schody.

8 Old Castle Steps
D2

The comparatively gentle slope of the Staré zámecké schody – the castle's "back door" entrance – leads from the Malostranská metro to the citadel's eastern gate. Local artists and artisans line the steps, selling

STAG MOAT

When the Stag Moat was not fulfilling its defensive duties, Prague's rulers used it as a hunting park. Rudolf II is said to have been particularly fond of chasing deer around the narrow, wooded gorge with his pet lions. The Powder Bridge's earthworks were excavated to permit pedestrians access to both halves of the moat.

everything from watercolour prints to polished stones.

9 Hradčanské náměstí
☑ B2

Many visitors enter this square backwards, trying to fit St Vitus's spires into their photographs. Tear your eyes away from the castle's western face and you'll see, among other Renaissance buildings, the colourful Archbishop's Palace and the Schwarzenberg Palace opposite, housing the Bohemian Baroque art of the National Gallery. In the green centre is a plague column from 1726; opposite the castle is the Toskánský Palace, now part of the Ministry of Foreign Affairs.

10 Schwarzenberg Palace
☑ B2

An inherent part of the Prague Castle panorama, Schwarzenberg Palace is a significant Early Renaissance building. Its façade is elaborately decorated with *sgraffito* patterns. The permanent exhibition here presents a selection of excellent masterpieces from the Old Masters collection.

**Small cottages on
Nový Svět in Hradčany**

A DAY IN HRADČANY

Morning

Start your day with a brisk climb up the **New Castle Steps**, then take a leisurely stroll through the grounds. When you're ready, leave the castle behind and walk west through **Hradčanské náměstí**; time your exit for the Changing of the Guard at noon. Next, head to the **Schwarzenberg Palace** and take time to browse some Baroque Czech art. Alternatively, treat yourself to the Old Masters collection at **Sternberg Palace**.

Afterwards, walk up **Loretánská** to **Loretánské náměstí**, where you'll find the vast **Černín Palace** staring down at **Loreta** (p34). Explore the pilgrimage site and its odd gallery of saints before having lunch at **Kavárna Nový Svět** (p108).

Afternoon

Exit Loretánské náměstí past the Capuchin monastery and follow Černínská downhill, pausing on **Nový Svět** lane. Admire the street's charming piebald houses and follow Kanovnická street back to Hradčanské náměstí.

The rest of the afternoon will be taken up with a tour of the unmissable **Prague Castle** (p22), **St Vitus Cathedral** (p26) and other attractions in the castle complex.

To end your sightseeing day in Hradčany, find your way back to the famed pub **U Černého vola** (p108) at Loretánské náměstí 1 for a generous mug of beer.

Cafés and Pubs

1. U Černého vola
🏠 A2 🚪 Loretánské nám. 1

"At the Black Ox" is one of the original Old Prague beerhalls. Watching the regulars knock back litres of beer, you can guess why it's so popular.

2. Pivovar Strahov
🏠 A3 🚪 Strahovské nádvoří 301

Located in the Strahov Monastery founded by Vladislav II in 1142, this place brews three unfiltered, unpasteurised beers on tap year-round.

3. Mandlárna
🏠 B2 🚪 Loretánská 5
🌐 loretanska.mandlarna.cz

Besides its delicious almond recipes, this café has everything from syrups and pastries to liquor. Try the speciality *Mandlokáva*, espresso with almonds.

4. Starbucks Pražský hrad
🏠 B2 🚪 Hradčanské náměstí - Kajetánka

Sip an espresso on the rooftop while peering at Prague through one of the telescopes. The quiet patio has large tables where you can enjoy lunch.

5. Kavárna Nový Svět
🏠 A2 🚪 Nový Svět 2 🌐 kavarna.novysvet.net

At this small family café, try soup or salad for lunch, or just sit with a good cup of coffee and enjoy the atmosphere.

6. Romantik Hotel U Raka
🏠 A2 🚪 Černínská 10

The Hotel U Raka at the far western end of Nový Svět is a striking half-timbered building, an unusual sight in the urban Czech Republic. Enjoy a coffee in cosy surroundings.

7. Mezi řádky
🏠 B2 🚪 Hradčanské nám. 15

Situated in the Sternberg Palace, this is a good spot to enjoy a cup of coffee and a light snack after visiting the castle.

8. Gallery Café
🏠 B2 🚪 U Prašného mostu 53

This café and gallery is situated at the Powder Bridge in the former Jízdárna (Riding School) building. Outdoor seating is available. Visitors can enjoy stunning views of the Stag Moat *(p106)*.

9. Café Melvin
🏠 A3 🚪 Pohořelec 8

Set in a 15th-century house at the beginning of the Royal Route, this café serves a range of beverages, home-made desserts and sandwiches.

10. Lobkowicz Palace Café
🏠 C2 🚪 Jiřshá 3 🌐 lobkowicz.cz

This pleasant restaurant offers light lunches and suppers with a view of the city. The café in the courtyard is a good place to end your tour of the castle.

Outdoor terrace of the Lobkowicz Palace Café

Restaurants

PRICE CATEGORIES
For a three-course meal for one with half a bottle of wine (or equivalent meal), taxes and extra charges

Ⓚ under Kč500   ⓀⓀ Kč500–Kč1,000
ⓀⓀⓀ over Kč1,000

Traditional Czech dishes
at Kuchyň

1. U Krále Brabantského
🅖 C2 🄰 Thunovská 15 🆆 hrcma
brabant.cz · ⓀⓀ
Meat lovers will enjoy this medieval-themed restaurant in a genuinely historic setting.

2. Na Pekle
🅖 A3 🄰 Strahovské nadvoří 1
🆆 napehle.cz · ⓀⓀ
Continental dining in a grotto under the Strahov Monastery. Traditional Czech meals include golden-roasted pork knee.

3. Vinobona
🅖 B2 🄰 Nový Svět 11
🆆 vinobona.cz · ⓀⓀⓀ
Set in the enchanting Nový Svět (p106), this bistro is a must-visit. It has delicious breakfast and lunch choices. The chef's degustation menu is great too, and there's an excellent choice of wines.

4. U ševce Matouše
🅖 A2 🄰 Loretánské náměstí 4
🆆 usevcematouse.cz · ⓀⓀ
"At the Cobbler Matouš", in a cosy, low, vaulted room, has made an art of melting cheese on beefsteaks.

5. Malý Buddha
🅖 A3 🄰 Úvoz 46 🆆 maly
buddha.cz · ⓀⓀ
The "Little Buddha" serves a wide range of potent teas and Vietnamese food.

6. Plzeňka Nový Svět
🅖 B2 🄰 Nový Svět 77 ☎ 773
781010 · ⓀⓀ
This restaurant serves delicious Czech and international dishes, and is immensely popular with locals and tourists alike.

7. Kuchyň
🅖 B2 🄰 Hradčanské náměstí 1
🆆 kuchyn.ambi.cz · ⓀⓀⓀ
Located in the Neo-Renaissance Schwarzenberg Palace (p107), Kuchyň offers homemade Czech meals inspired by recipes from old cookbooks along with excellent tank beer.

8. U Labutí
🅖 B2 🄰 Hradčanské náměstí 11
🆆 ulabuti.com · ⓀⓀ
Restaurant "At the Swans" serves up Zubr lager and some substantial dishes, such as schnitzel and goulash. There is seating in the courtyard.

9. Host Restaurant
🅖 B2 🄰 Loretánská 15 🆆 restaurant
host.cz · ⓀⓀⓀ
Enjoy fine dining alongside sweeping views of Petřín Hill and Malá Strana.

10. Lví dvůr
🅖 B1 🄰 U Prašného mostu 6
🆆 restaurant-lvidvur.cz · ⓀⓀ
This rooftop dining room affords great views of St Vitus Cathedral (p26). Enjoy Lobkowicz Premium beer alongside delicious Czech cuisine.

Clockwise from above
Overlooking Prague from the steps under Prague Castle; tourists climbing the Old Castle Steps; statue of Karel Hašler "The Songster" by Stanislav Hanzík

JOSEFOV AND NORTHERN STARÉ MĚSTO

It is impossible to precisely date the arrival of the Jewish community in Prague, but historical sources mention the destruction of a Jewish settlement on the Vltava's left bank in the 13th century. For the next 500 years, Prague's Jewish population was obliged to live in a walled ghetto, where the Josefov quarter is today. When Emperor Josef II removed these strictures, the ghetto turned into a slum occupied by the city's poorest population. The quarter was razed in the late 19th century, making way for avenues such as Pařížská. Now the area is home to the Jewish Museum, which showcases Prague's Jewish heritage.

Gravestones in the
Old Jewish Cemetery

1 Old Jewish Cemetery

K2 🏛 **Široká** ⏰ **Apr–Oct: 9am–6pm Sun–Fri; Nov–Mar: 9am–4:30pm Sun–Fri** 🌐 **jewishmuseum.cz** ⚡

The sight of hundreds of graves, their leaning headstones crumbling on top of each other, is a moving and unforgettable experience – a testament to the treatment of the Jewish people in Prague, confined to their own ghetto even in death. Although there is no definite record of the number of burial sites located here, to appreciate the depth of the graveyard, compare the gravestones' height with that of the street level on U Starého hřbitova.

2 Spanish Synagogue

M2 🏛 **Vézeňská 1** ⏰ **Apr–Oct: 9am–6pm Sun–Fri; Nov–Mar: 9am–4:30pm Sun–Fri** ⚡

The Moorish interior with its swirling arabesques and stucco decoration gives this synagogue *(p51)* its name. It stands on the site of the Old School, Prague's first Jewish house of worship. František Škroup, composer of the Czech national anthem, was the organist in the mid-19th century. It hosts exhibitions of Jewish history and synagogue silver.

Arabesque façade of the
Spanish Synagogue

Jewish exhibits,
Klausen Synagogue

3 Klausen Synagogue

K2 **U Starého hřbitova 1** **Apr–Oct: 9am–6pm Sun–Fri; Nov–Mar: 9am–4:30pm Sun–Fri**

Abutting the Old Jewish Cemetery, this Baroque building was constructed in 1694 on the site of a school and prayer hall (*klausen*) where Rabbi Loew taught the *cabala*. It now houses Jewish exhibits, including prints and manuscripts.

4 Maisel Synagogue

L3 **Maiselova 10** **Apr–Oct: 9am–6pm Sun–Fri; Nov–Mar: 9am–4:30pm Sun–Fri**

Rudolf II permitted Mordechai Maisel to build his private synagogue here in the late 16th century, in gratitude for the Jewish mayor's financial help during Bohemia's war against the Turks. It was destroyed by fire in 1689, but was later rebuilt as a Jewish museum (*p36*) in Neo-Gothic style. Inside is a wonderful collection of Jewish silverwork and other items such as candlesticks and ceramics. Ironically, during the Nazi occupation, the Third Reich planned to build a museum in Prague, dedicated to the Jewish people as an "extinct race".

RABBI JUDAH LOEW BEN BEZALEL

One of Prague's most famed residents, Rabbi Loew ben Bezalel (c 1520–1609) is associated with numerous local legends but he was also a pioneering pedagogue and a leading Hebrew scholar of the times.

Foremost among the myths surrounding Loew is that of the Golem (*p60*), a clay automaton the rabbi supposedly created to defend the ghetto.

---

5 Ceremonial Hall

K2 **U Starého hřbitova 3a** **Apr–Oct: 9am–6pm Sun–Fri; Nov–Mar: 9am–4:30pm Sun–Fri**

Constructed in the early 1900s in striking mock Romanesque fashion, the Ceremonial Hall was home to the Jewish community's Burial Society. The fascinating exhibits housed inside detail the complex Jewish rituals for preparing the dead for the grave.

6 Pinkas Synagogue

K3 **Široká 3** **Apr–Oct: 9am–6pm Sun–Fri; Nov–Mar: 9am–4:30pm Sun–Fri**

After World War II, this 15th-century Gothic building with some early Renaissance features became a monument to the estimated 80,000 Czech and Moravian victims of the Holocaust – the names and dates of all those known to have died either in the Terezín camp or in others across Eastern Europe are written on the wall in a moving memorial. Equally moving is the exhibition of writings and paintings made by the children (of whom there were more than 10,000 under the age of 15) confined in Terezín (*p39*).

7 Old-New Synagogue

K2 **Červená** **Apr–Oct: 9am–6pm Sun–Fri; Nov–Mar: 9am–5pm Sun–Fri** **synagogue.cz**

Across the street from the cemetery, Europe's oldest surviving synagogue has witnessed a turbulent history, including pogroms and fire, and has

A DAY IN THE JEWISH QUARTER

St Agnes of Bohemia Convent

Old-New Synagogue

Spanish Synagogue

Klausen Synagogue

Old Jewish Cemetery

Bakeshop Praha

Pinkas Synagogue

Jewish Town Hall

Café Golem

5th District Restaurant and Café by King Solomon

Maisel Synagogue

Morning

A sobering place to start the day, the **Pinkas Synagogue** lists Holocaust victims and helps visitors to appreciate how large the Czech Jewish community once was. Afterwards take a stroll through the adjoining **Old Jewish Cemetery** (p113). Also worth visiting in this area is the Baroque **Klausen Synagogue**, with its exhibits on Jewish family life.

A short walk away is the **Old-New Synagogue**, where you'll find treasures like Rabbi Loew's seat. Exiting, note the **Jewish Town Hall** next door. Inside the Jewish Quarter information centre is **Café Golem** (p117), a good stop for a light lunch.

Afternoon

After lunch, enter antiques shops en route to the **Maisel Synagogue**, where you'll find an exhibit on the Jewish settlement in Bohemia and Moravia – it continues at the **Spanish Synagogue** a five-minute walk to the east down Široká.

Refresh yourself at **Bakeshop Praha** (p116) before walking a few minutes northeast to the **St Agnes of Bohemia Convent** (p40) with its exhibits on Czech medieval art.

Finally, enjoy dinner at **5th District Restaurant and Café by King Solomon** (p117) and attend a concert of sacred music at the Spanish Synagogue.

---

often been a place of refuge for the city's beleaguered Jewish community. Its name may come from the fact that another synagogue was built after this one, taking the title "new", but which was later destroyed.

8 Jewish Town Hall
L3 **Maiselova 18**
To the public

The hands of the Rococo clock on the town hall, or *Židovská radnice*, turn counterclockwise as Hebrew is read from right to left. The building was one of Mordechai Maisel's gifts to his community in the late 16th century, but it was renovated in Baroque style in 1763.

9 High Synagogue
L2 **Červená 4** **To the public**

Constructed along with the town hall with funds from Mordechai Maisel, the High Synagogue was built in elegant Renaissance fashion. Subsequent reconstructions updated the exterior, but the interior retains its original stucco vaults. Inside there are also impressive Torah scrolls and mantles.

10 St Agnes of Bohemia Convent

This 13th-century Gothic convent (p40) is full of spectacular wall panels and altarpieces, as well as original 13th-century cloisters and chapels. The artworks, part of the gallery's collection, comprise some of the best Czech medieval and early Renaissance art.

Shops

1. Spanish Synagogue Gift Shop
M2 ⊠ Vězeňská 1
Exquisite torah pointers, *kabala* hands, *Hannuka menoras* (nine-branched candelabrums) and books are all on offer at this shop.

2. Kosta Boda
L3 ⊠ Maiselova 12
The tiny Josefov outpost of the renowned glassmaker has been producing glass artworks and tablewares since the mid-1700s.

3. Hodinářství (Old Clocks)
L3 ⊠ Maiselova 16
To find this small shop selling old clocks, simply stand at the corner of Maiselova and Široká streets and you'll hear the old cuckoo clock sing.

4. Granát Turnov
N2 ⊠ Dlouhá 28
Specializing in Bohemian garnet, Granát Turnov is part of Prague's biggest jewellery chain. Jewellery lovers can find a large variety of brooches and necklaces here.

5. Gucci
L3 ⊠ Pařížshá 9
Treat yourself to high-end luxury fashion from this world-renowned brand. Located on the tree-lined Pařížská street, this store is one of many designer boutiques frequented by tourists and locals alike.

6. Drahonovsky
M2 ⊠ Dlouhá 19
Aficionados come to this tiny goldsmith's workshop for gold and silver jewellery, much of which is embellished with the celebrated red Bohemian garnet.

7. Bakeshop Praha
M2 ⊠ Kozí 1
Grab a bag of brownies, *rugelach* or butterhorns (small crescent-shaped

Baked treats at the Bakeshop Praha

biscuits) and other mouthwatering treats, or lunch on an egg salad sandwich and coffee. There are also salads and quiches to take away.

8. Antik Ambra
L3 ⊠ Kaprova 12
This serious collector's shop specializes in jewels and small decorative items such as clocks and coins. If you don't find what you're looking for, just ask and they'll point you in the right direction.

9. Antique Cinolter
L3 ⊠ Maiselova 9
Art lovers should peruse this small gallery's sale exhibition of local art. The original oils and sketches capture Josefov's bittersweet warmth and humanity.

10. Alma Antique
K3 ⊠ Valentinshá 7
What don't they sell? Alma Antique is a bazaar stocked with Persian rugs, jewellery, Meissen porcelain, crystal and ornate nesting dolls. This is one of the largest antique dealers in Prague.

Cafés and Restaurants

1. Krčma
L3 ⌂ Kostečná 4 📞 725 157262 · Ⓚ Ⓚ
A medieval-themed tavern just off swanky Pařížská, Krčma offers reasonably priced food, draught beer and lots of low-lit ambiance.

2. Naše maso
N2 ⌂ Dlouhá 39 · Ⓚ Ⓚ
The casual setting in a butcher shop makes this better suited to a quick bite. The meat is quality local beef and pork.

3. Field
M1 ⌂ U Milosrdných 12
🖥 fieldrestaurant.cz · Ⓚ Ⓚ Ⓚ
A stylish restaurant, with an intimate atmosphere and an interesting mural projected from the ceiling. Innovative dishes and modern cuisine are served.

4. La Degustation Bohême Bourgeoise
N2 ⌂ Haštalská 18
🖥 ladegustation.cz · Ⓚ Ⓚ Ⓚ
La Degustation, a Michelin-starred restaurant, offers tasting menus of traditional Czech cuisine.

5. La Bodeguita del Medio
K3 ⌂ Kaprova 5
🖥 labodeguita.com · Ⓚ Ⓚ
This Cuban-Creole restaurant offers grilled fish and meats made using traditional ingredients. Popular with the business crowd, it has a great atmosphere and welcoming staff.

5th District Restaurant
and Café by King Solomon

PRICE CATEGORIES

For a three-course meal for one with half a bottle of wine (or equivalent meal), taxes and extra charges

Ⓚ under Kč500　Ⓚ Ⓚ Kč500–Kč1,000
Ⓚ Ⓚ Ⓚ over Kč1,000

6. Pivnice u Pivrnce
L3 ⌂ Maiselova 3
🖥 upivrnce.cz · Ⓚ Ⓚ
A pub with wall decorations by Czech caricaturist Peter Urban. Choose from Czech specialities or enjoy a beer.

7. La Finestra in Cucina
K4 ⌂ Platnéřská 13　🖥 lafinestra. lacollezione.cz · Ⓚ Ⓚ Ⓚ
Italian favourites cooked to perfection and great wine are complemented by the fine setting and service.

8. Les Moules
L2 ⌂ Pařížská 19
🖥 lesmoules.cz · Ⓚ Ⓚ
Enjoy oysters and mussels at this Belgian restaurant.

9. Café Golem
L3 ⌂ Maiselova 15 📞 603 962963 · Ⓚ
This stylish little café serves great coffee, bagels, soups and cakes.

10. 5th District Restaurant and Café by King Solomon
L3 ⌂ Široká 8 🕐 Fri
🖥 patactvrt.cz · Ⓚ Ⓚ Ⓚ
Prague's foremost kosher restaurant has separate facilities for meat and dairy.

NOVÉ MĚSTO

Founded in 1348, Nové Město (New Town) is hardly new. Charles IV's urban development scheme imposed straight avenues on the settlements springing up outside the old city walls and added a fourth town to the constellation of Staré Město, Malá Strana and Hradčany. Unlike Staré Město, Nové Město was a planned grid of streets and markets. The horse market became Wenceslas Square in the 19th century; the 14th-century cattle market, and Europe's largest square, took on Charles's name, becoming Karlovo náměstí.

1 Top 10 Sights
p119

1 Restaurants
p125

1 Cafés and pubs
p124

1 Galleries
p122

1 Nightspots
p123

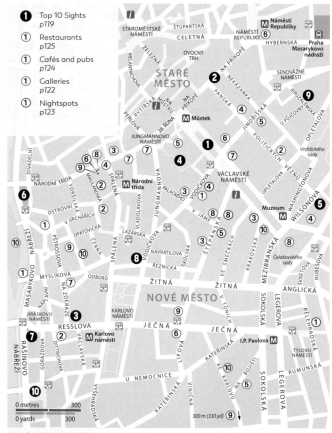

For places to stay in this area, see p146

Wenceslas Square, Prague's bustling commercial hub

1 Wenceslas Square

Standing in contrast to the medieval Old Town Square *(p28)*, the lively Wenceslas Square *(p42)* expresses the history of 20th-century Prague, from its many beautiful Art Nouveau façades to the memories of the numerous marches, political protests and celebrations that have shaped the city over the past 100 years.

2 Na Příkopě
☑ N5

Formerly a moat protecting the city's eastern flank, Na Příkopě is Prague's fashion boulevard, counting Gant, Benetton, Desigual and Guess among its range of big-name stores. Shoppers jam the pedestrian zone and pavement cafés, streaming between the gleaming Myslbek shopping centre and Slovanský dům, with its ten-screen multiplex cinema. The Hussite firebrand Jan Želivský preached on the site now occupied by another shopping mall, the Černá Růže Palace.

3 Cathedral of Sts Cyril and Methodius
☑ E5 ☑ Resslova 9 ☑ 9am–5pm Tue–Sun

This Baroque church, with a pilastered façade and a small central tower, was built in the 1730s. In the 1930s, the church was given to the Czechoslovak Orthodox Church and dedicated to Sts Cyril and St Methodius, the 9th-century "Apostles to the Slavs". In 1942, the Heydrich Terror *(p51)* took place here. A small museum on-site tells the story of these events. In the crypt is the National Memorial to the Heroes of the Heydrich Terror – a bronze plaque has been hung on the wall in their memory.

4 Franciscan Garden
☑ N6

The Franciscans moved here in 1604, claiming a former Carmelite monastery. The grounds and nearby Church of Our Lady of the Snows had fallen into decay after the Hussite civil war, but the monks beautifully restored them. The area was closed to the public until 1950, when the Communists thought the gardens were worth sharing. Although there's little love lost for the dictatorship of the proletariat, the garden *(p43)* remains popular with locals.

Heydrich Terror memorial, Cathedral of Sts Cyril and Methodius

5 State Opera

📍 G4 🏛 Wilsonova 4
🌐 narodni-divadlo.cz

The first theatre built here, the New Town Theatre, was pulled down in 1885 to make way for the present building. A Neo-Classical frieze decorates the pediment above the columned loggia at the front of the theatre. The interior is stuccoed, and original paintings in the auditorium and on the curtain have been preserved.

6 National Theatre

📍 E4 🏛 Národní třída 2
🌐 narodni-divadlo.cz

Patriotic Czechs funded the theatre's construction twice: once in 1868 and again after fire destroyed the building in 1883. To see the stunning allegorical ceiling frescoes and Vojtěch Hynais's celebrated stage curtain, take in one of the operas staged here; good picks are Smetana's *Libuše*, which debuted here, or Dvořák's *The Devil and Kate*. You can see multimedia performances at The New Stage (p72) next door.

7 Dancing House

📍 E6 🏛 Jiráskovo náměstí 6
🌐 galerietancicidum.cz

Built in 1992–6, this edifice by Vlado Milunic and Frank Gehry is known as the Dancing House, or "Ginger and Fred", due to its iconic towers, which resemble two dancers. Most of the building is now a hotel owned by former Czech international football player, Vladimír Šmicer. The two tower rooms, with their castle and Vltava views, are among the best in the capital.

8 New Town Hall

📍 F5 🏛 Karlovo náměstí 1
🕐 Tower: 10am–6pm Tue–Sun
🌐 nrpraha.cz 🚻

In 1419, an anti-clerical mob led by Jan Želivský hurled the Catholic mayor and his councillors from a New Town Hall window in the first of Prague's defenestrations (p25). The Gothic tower was added a few years later; its viewing platform is open to the public. Crowds of locals gather at the tower's base most Saturdays to congratulate newlyweds married in the building's Gothic hall.

MŮSTEK

The area at the bottom of Wenceslas Square takes its name from the "Little Bridge" that spanned the moat here in medieval times. Below the surface, at the top of the escalators descending to the train platform, you'll find the remains of that bridge, uncovered by workers building the metro.

The Dancing House, nicknamed "Ginger and Fred"

9 Jerusalem Synagogue

🅓 G3 🅐 Jeruzalémská 7 🅞 9am–6pm Sun–Fri 🅦 synagogue.cz/en/jerusalem-synagogue

Built between 1896 and 1906, this is Prague's youngest synagogue and perhaps its most striking. Architect Wilhelm Stiassny blended Moorish revival and Art Nouveau styling throughout the exterior and interior, to stunning effect. Two towers flank the horseshoe arch on the coloured façade, while the interior is decorated with rich colours and grand chandeliers, which dangle above the 850-seat space below.

10 Palackého náměstí

🅓 E6

The riverside square is named for the 19th-century historian František Palacký, whose work was integral to the National Revival. Stanislav Sucharda's sweeping monument to him stands at the plaza's northern end, while the modern steeples of the Emmaus Monastery (p61) rise from the eastern edge. The church grounds are also known as the Slavonic Monastery.

František Palacký Monument on Palackého náměstí

A DAY IN NOVÉ MĚSTO

Morning

Head to **Wenceslas Square** (p42) to begin the day's sightseeing. Start with the **National Museum** (p122) at the top of the square, if only to see the marble stairway, the Pantheon and the city views from the dome. Walk to **St Wenceslas's Statue** and the monument to the victims of Communist rule. Enjoy a bit of retail therapy as you stroll northwest to Můstek, then visit the **Museum of Communism** (p122), or peacefully stroll through the **Franciscan Garden** (p119). Then walk ten minutes west down stately Národní třída towards the river for lunch at **Café Louvre** (p124).

Afternoon

A short walk to the river and north along its banks leads you to the **National Theatre** for a glimpse at its magnificent façade. Then follow the Vltava south. Modern art buffs should stop at **Galerie Mánes** (p122) on the way. Further south, pause at Jiráskovo náměstí to admire the iconic **Dancing House**. Then turn left and follow Resslova uphill to the **Cathedral of Sts Cyril and Methodius** (p119).

Take in a performance at the National Theatre in the evening; **U Fleků** (p124) is the obvious choice for dinner. Then, head to **Radost FX** (p123) to dance the night away or to **Rocky O'Reilly's** (p123) for its cosy atmosphere and live music.

Galleries and Museums

1. Galerie Mánes
⊡ E5 ⌂ Masarykovo nábřeží 250 ⊙ Hours vary, chech website ⊠ ncvu.eu ⚡

Occupying the southern tip of Žofín Island, this contemporary art gallery hosts both Czech and foreign artists.

2. Galerie Via Art
⊡ E6 ⌂ Resslova 6 ⊙ 1–5pm Mon–Fri ⊠ galerieviaart.com

Founded in 1991 as one of Prague's first private galleries, Galerie Via Art exhibits contemporary painting, sculpture and mixed-media art.

3. Lego Museum
⊡ L6 ⌂ Národní 31 ⊙ 10am–8pm daily ⊠ muzeumlega.cz

This Lego Museum is among the largest in the world. It may essentially be a gift shop with a museum attached, but the impressive Lego sculptures and interactive models will keep the kids entertained.

4. Mucha Museum
⊡ P5 ⌂ Panská 7 ⊙ 10am–6pm daily ⊠ mucha.cz ⚡

Art Nouveau artist Alfons Mucha is a celebrated figure in the country. Here you'll find his journals, sketchbooks and paintings, both private and commercial.

5. Museum of Senses
⊡ P5 ⌂ Jindřišská 20 ⊙ 10am–10pm daily ⊠ muzeumsmyslu.cz

This interactive museum has over 50 fun and engaging exhibits, including incredible optical illusions.

6. Museum of Communism
⊡ P3 ⌂ V Celnici 4 ⊙ 9am–8pm daily ⊠ muzeumkomunismu.cz ⚡

A triptych of the dream, reality and nightmare that was Communist Czechoslovakia. The museum is filled with mementos.

7. Václav Špála Gallery
⊡ L6 ⌂ Národní 30 ⊙ 11am–7pm daily ⊠ galerievaclava spaly.cz

This contemporary gallery exhibits works mainly by local artists and aims to make art more accessible.

8. National Museum
The collection across the two linked sites (*p44*) is mainly devoted to archaeology, anthropology, mineralogy, numismatics and natural history. But it also includes several excellent exhibitions on Prague and Czech history.

9. Police Museum
⊡ G7 ⌂ Ke Karlovu 1 ⊙ 10am–5pm Tue–Sun ⊠ muzeumpolicie.cz ⚡

Engaging exhibits, such as an interactive crime scene, document the history of the police in Prague.

10. Dvořák Museum
⊡ G6 ⌂ Ke Karlovu 20 ⊙ 10am–5pm Tue–Sun ⊠ nm.cz ⚡

This Baroque palace houses Antonín Dvořák's (*p57*) piano and viola, as well as other memorabilia.

Stained glass, Mucha Museum

Partygoers at Zone, a popular cocktail bar

Nightspots

1. Radost FX
G6 ⬛ Bělehradská 120 🌐 radostfx.cz
Late at night, club kids take over the disco and lounge of this popular club. Eclectic music is paired with imaginative light shows, video projections, dancers and regular sets by the best local and international DJs.

2. Balbi Bar
E4 ⬛ Mikulandská 6 🌐 balbi bar.com
Excellent cocktails, welcoming staff and a cosy atmosphere make this bar the perfect place to spend an evening.

3. Nebe Cocktail & Music Bar
G4 ⬛ Václavské náměstí 56
This bar has over 100 delicious cocktails to choose from. Relax with a drink under the vaulted ceilings, or dance the night away to a mix of current pop and R&B hits, as well as music from the 1980s and 90s.

4. Lucerna Music Bar
N6 ⬛ Vodičkova 36 🌐 musicbar.cz
The granddaddy of Prague's clubs, the cavernous Lucerna hosts concerts as well as rock and dance parties.

5. Rocky O'Reilly's
F5 ⬛ Štěpánská 32 🌐 rochyoreillys.cz
Offering all a Celtophile could ask for, this pub has live music in the evenings, football on the TV, a roaring fire and plenty of stout. The food here is decent.

6. Reduta Jazz Club
L6 ⬛ Národní 20 🌐 reduta jazzclub.cz
Many celebrated musicians have played here, as has former US President Bill Clinton. Visit to hear all types of jazz from swing bands to modern styles.

7. Duplex Club
N6 ⬛ Václavské náměstí 21
During the day, Duplex is an ideal location for lunch or dinner with good views of the city. At night it turns into one of Prague's most exclusive clubs.

8. Alcron Bar
G4 ⬛ Štěpánská 40
Set in the luxurious Almanac X Alcron hotel, this Art Deco-style elegant bar offers a wide range of unique signature cocktails, drinks and delicious snacks.

9. Rock Café
L6 ⬛ Národní 20 🌐 rochcafe.cz
Conveniently set in the heart of the city, Rock Café hosts live concerts and has a multimedia space that features a theatre and a gallery.

10. Zone
E5 ⬛ Křemencova 10 🌐 zonebar.cz
This atmospheric club in an original stone cellar features stylish lighting and a gracefully curvaceous long bar. There's a separate lounge too, which is a popular place for private events.

Cafés and Pubs

Art Nouveau interior of
Kavárna Lucerna

1. Kavárna Lucerna
Q N6 **Q** Vodičkova 36 **W** kavarna.
lucerna.cz

This stylish "Lantern" café is the ideal place to enjoy coffee before watching a film or dancing at the nearby club.

2. La Casa de la Havana vieja
Q E4 **Q** Opatovická 28
W casahavana.cz

A classic Cuban cocktail bar, this spot captures the vibe of 1930s Cuba, offering a family-friendly atmosphere.

3. Café 35mm
Q F5 **Q** Štěpánská 35

Students at the Institut Français and other Francophones gather here for coffee, quiche or a croissant.

4. Pilsnerka Národní
Q E4 **Q** Národní 22 **W** pilsnerka
narodni.cz

This is one of the best places to enjoy Pilsner Urquell. Try their tappings – milk, *šnyt* (cut) and *hladinka* (level).

5. Hospoda U Kalicha
Q G6 **Q** Na bojišti 12–14 **W** ukalicha.cz

This pub's decor and cartooned walls are based on the Czech novel *The Good*

Soldier Švejk. Author Jaroslav Hašek *(p56)* set some of the pivotal scenes here.

6. Pivovarský dům
Q F6 **Q** Ječná 16 **W** pivo-dum.cz

A lovely restaurant and brewery, with traditional Czech interiors, which offers a unique range of beers.

7. Kavárna Adria
Q M6 **Q** Národní 36

This café offers excellent coffee and homemade cakes.

8. Café Louvre
Q L6 **Q** Národní 22 **W** cafelouvre.cz

Franz Kafka, Max Brod and their writer friends used to hold court here. It's a bright, cheerful place, good for conversation and grabbing a bite to eat.

9. U Fleků
Q E5 **Q** Křemencova 11 **W** en.ufleku.cz

U Fleků is the city's oldest brewing pub, dating to 1499, and probably the most popular, and the reasonable prices reflect it. It is known for its dark lager.

10. Oliver's Coffee Cup
Q G4 **Q** Václavské náměstí 58
W oliverscoffeecup.cz

Named after the founder's sons, both called Oliver, this cosy café offers a variety of caffeinated drinks, all served by polite and attentive staff.

U Fleků, Prague's
famous beer hall

Restaurants

1. U Zpěváčků
🅟 E5 ⌂ Na Struze 7
ⓦ uzpevachu.com · ⓀⓀ
Established in 1865, this restaurant
is known for its beer and homemade
Czech cuisine.

2. Restaurace Bredovský dvůr
🅟 P6 ⌂ Politických vězňů 13
ⓦ restauracebredovskydvur.cz · ⓀⓀ
Enjoy traditional Czech dishes such as
game goulash with Carlsbad dumplings.
In the summer, you can eat alfresco.

3. Namaste India Palackého
🅟 F4 ⌂ Palackého 15 ⓦ namaste
india.cz · ⓀⓀ
Come here for tasty, traditional Indian
cuisine. The restaurant offers an all-
you-can-eat buffet.

4. Čestr
🅟 G4 ⌂ Legerova 75 ⓦ cestr.
ambi.cz · ⓀⓀⓀ
Meat lovers will get a real kick out of
this top-notch smokehouse restaurant,
where cuts of beef and pork are cooked
to perfection.

5. U Pinkasů
🅟 M6 ⌂ Jungmannovo náměstí 16
☎ 221 111152 · ⓀⓀ
A great-value Czech beer hall since
1843, this is a very popular lunchtime
destination. Food is simple but hearty.

6. Modrý Zub
🅟 N6 ⌂ Jindřišská 5 ⓦ modryzub.
com · ⓀⓀ
This is fast Thai food at its best, great
for a quick snack or light meal. Huge

**Old-fashioned Czech
pub-restaurant U Šumavy**

windows create a great opportunity
for people watching.

7. Lemon Leaf
🅟 E5 ⌂ Myslíkova 14 ⓦ lemon.cz · ⓀⓀ
There's a wide array of Thai and
Continental dishes. The ingredients
used are fresh, the presentation colour-
ful and service is fast and friendly.

8. Jáma³ Garden Pub
🅟 F4 ⌂ V jámě 7 ⓦ jamagarden
pub.cz · ⓀⓀ
Delicious Tex-Mex and American
specialities and a fun atmosphere.
Jáma organizes regular parties
and sports events.

9. U Šumavy
🅟 E5 ⌂ Štěpánshá 3
ⓦ usumavy.cz · ⓀⓀ
This old-fashioned pub restaurant
is a little piece of the Czech countryside in central Prague. The food
is traditional – most meals are
served with dumplings.

10. Žofin Garden
🅟 E5 ⌂ Slovanshý ostrov 8
ⓦ zofinrestaurant.cz · ⓀⓀⓀ
Near the National Theatre
on Slav Island, this restaurant
serves elevated takes on traditional Czech game dishes at
reasonable prices.

GREATER PRAGUE

Prague's city centre can keep most visitors occupied for days, but if you're staying outside the city's heart, or if you have the time to explore beyond the capital's walls, the outlying areas offer plenty of surprises. Over the centuries, the various rulers of Prague have used the surrounding countryside as their personal playground, building impressive castles, palaces and parks to which they could escape the often claustrophobic streets and winding alleyways of the city. Even the Communists have left their own kind of functional mark on the area, with useful edifices, towers and exhibition spaces. From the peaceful parklands of Vyšehrad and the social atmosphere of Letná, to the noisy nightlife of Žižkov and the intriguing gardens of Holešovice and Troja, Greater Prague has a diversity that will fulfil almost any requirements you might have.

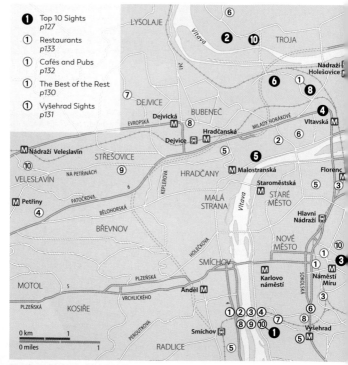

1	Top 10 Sights *p127*
1	Restaurants *p133*
1	Cafés and Pubs *p132*
1	The Best of the Rest *p130*
1	Vyšehrad Sights *p131*

For places to stay in this area, see p147

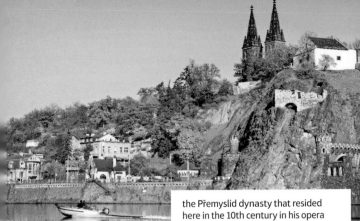

Historic Vyšehrad complex above the Vltava river

1 Vyšehrad

🔲 R3

The former fortress of Vyšehrad is steeped in legend. Bedřich Smetana paid tribute to the second seat of the Přemyslid dynasty that resided here in the 10th century in his opera *Libuše* and in his rousing work *Má vlast (p57)*. He is buried here in the National Cemetery, which is also home to the Slavín Monument *(p131)*.

2 Prague Zoo

🔲 R1 🏛 U Trojského zámku 3, Troja 🕐 Hours vary, chech website 🌐 zoopraha.cz

This zoo is the second most popular attraction in the country after Prague Castle. Spread across a vast area, it is home to numerous bird and animal species, including elephants, gorillas and giant salamanders.

3 Vinohrady

🔲 S2

Originally the royal vineyards, Vinohrady today is a gently rolling residential neighbourhood. The central square, Náměstí Míru, features the Neo-Gothic Church of St Ludmila and the Art Nouveau Vinohrady Theatre. For a bit of peace and greenery, visit Havlíčkovy sady.

4 Holešovice

🔲 R1

Home to the National Gallery's Trade Fair Palace *(p54)*, which holds the gallery's collection of modern and contemporary art, this once-bustling warehouse district is being redeveloped to make a comeback. Motorcar enthusiasts will love the National Technical Museum *(p55)*, with its exhibits of Czech interwar vehicles such as Škodas, as well as other vintage vehicles.

5 Letná Park
E1

A grand staircase leads from the Vltava riverbank opposite the Josefov quarter *(p112)* to a giant metronome. Prior to this oversized timekeeper, a mammoth stone statue of Joseph Stalin stood on the plinth here, but it was blown up in 1962. The surrounding wooded park echoes with the clatter of skateboards and barking dogs. Travelling circuses sometimes set up in the open fields, but Letná's biggest draw is probably its popular beer garden, which is found at the garden's eastern end.

6 Stromovka
R1

King Ottokar II established the royal game park here in the 13th century; it's been a public garden since 1804 (*stromovka* means "place of trees"). Stroll or skate through the ancient park *(p67)* by day and visit the planetarium by night. The fish ponds were a creation of Rudolf II – the emperor drilled a tunnel under Letná in the 16th century to bring in water to supply them.

7 Žižkov TV Tower
S2 **Mahlerovy sady 1** **9am–midnight** **towerpark.cz**

The Prague TV Tower is the highest building in Prague, reaching 216 m (709 ft) in height. However it didn't begin transmitting until after the Velvet Revolution *(p11)*. Three thematically different "capsules" at the tower offer unforgettable views of the city, especially at sunset. Outside the tower, there are ten giant sculptures of babies by Czech artist David Černý.

ŽIŽKOV

This neighbourhood came into existence when the city founders divided the Královské Vinohrady district. The inhabitants of the area thumbed their noses at Habsburg rule and named their new district after the Hussite warrior. Žižkovites' contrary nature runs deep, even having a separatist movement which promotes an independent Republic of Žižkov. An alternative culture thrives around the Akropolis club and the Divus artists collective.

8 Výstaviště
R1

Originally built at the end of the 19th century to host trade shows, this exhibition ground is like nothing else in Prague. Although large parts of the complex are currently being renovated, including the Křižík fountain and the Lapidárium *(p130)*, the area is still worth a visit on a rainy day for the country's largest aquarium, Mořský Svět. There's also an indoor swimming pool and an ice-hockey rink. The exterior of the Art Nouveau-style Industrial Palace is also a sight to behold.

Enjoying drinks in
Letná's beer garden

9 National Memorial on the Vítkov Hill

📍S2 🚇Žižkov 🕐10am–6pm
Wed–Sun 🌐nm.cz ♿

The one-eyed Hussite general
Jan Žižka defeated invading
crusaders in 1420 atop the hill
where his giant equestrian statue
now stands in front of the Tomb
of the Unknown Soldier. Erected
in 1929, the monument serves as
a memorial to all those who
suffered in the Czech struggle
for independence. The Communists
co-opted the building, and for a
time it served as President Klement
Gottwald's mausoleum.

10 Troja Château

📍R1 🚌U Trojského
zámku 1, Troja 🕐Apr–Oct:
10am–6pm Tue–Thu, Sat &
Sun; 1–6pm Fri 🌐ghmp.cz ♿

One of the most striking
summer palaces in Prague,
Troja Château was built in the
late 17th century by Jean-Baptiste
Mathey for Count Sternberg. Surrounded by beautiful gardens and
two orangeries, the château has
a good collection of 19th-century
art and sculpture.

Troja Château surrounded
by pretty gardens

THREE AFTERNOON WALKS

Afternoon One

See **Vyšehrad** (p127) late in the
day, but only if the weather looks
promising. Take the metro to the
Vyšehrad stop at the **Congress
Centre** (p131), from where you have
marvellous views of Prague's spires.
Walk west along Na Bučance and
enter the fortifications through
the **Tábor Gate** (p131). Once
inside the walls, you'll find historic
constructions everywhere, such
as the lovely Romanesque
Rotunda of St Martin (p131).
Enjoy the park at your leisure but
get to the westernmost edge of
the compound atop Vyšehrad's
rocky outcrop in time for sunset.

Afternoon Two

Žižkov and **Vinohrady** (p127) are
also best seen in the second half
of the day. From Florenc metro,
climb to the **National Memorial
on the Vítkov Hill** for a wonderful
view, then compare it to the one
you get from the **Žižkov TV
Tower**. Take a stroll as far into
Vinohrady as your feet will permit
you, but save your strength: you'll
need it for a night out clubbing.

Afternoon Three

Energetic and keen walkers can
manage to see **Stromovka** and
Troja in half a day. Take the tram
to **Výstaviště**, before crossing
the Vltava to the **Troja Château**.
From there, you're within easy
walking distance of **Prague Zoo**
(p127). Take bus 112 back to the
metro at Nádraží Holešovice.

The Best of the Rest

1. Lapidárium
◉ B5 ⬠ Výstaviště 422, Holešovice
◷ For renovation ⬡ nm.cz ✦
Several statues including the Marian column from Old Town Square *(p28)* and sculptures from Charles Bridge *(p32)* are on display here.

2. National Museum of Agriculture
◉ B5 ⬠ Kostelní 44, Holešovice
◷ 9am–5pm Tue–Sun ⬡ nzm.cz ✦
A visit to this museum is an excursion through Czech agricultural history.

3. The City of Prague Museum
◉ H2 ⬠ Na Poříčí 52 ◷ 9am–6pm Tue–Sun ⬡ en.muzeumprahy.cz ✦
Visitors can explore the history of Prague at this museum.

4. Břevnov Monastery
◉ Q2 ⬠ Markétská 1, Břevnov ◷ Hours vary, chech website ⬡ brevnov.cz ✦
St Adalbert founded this Benedictine monastery in 993. You can see the remains of a Romanesque, 18th-century church

5. Bílek Villa
◉ D1 ⬠ Michiewiczova 1, Hradčany
◷ 10am–6pm Tue–Sun ⬡ ghmp.cz ✦
The exhibition of art at this villa captures the essence and style of František Bílek's body of work and techniques.

6. Olšany Cemetery
◉ S2 ⬠ Vinohradshá 153 ◷ Mar, Apr, Oct: 8am–6pm daily; May–Sep 8am–7pm daily; Nov–Feb: 8am–5pm daily
Many notable Czech personalities, such as Jan Palach *(p43)* are buried in this vast cemetery. Visitors can get a free map at the entrance.

7. Kafka's Grave
◉ C6 ⬠ Izraelshá 1 ◷ 9am–5pm Sun–Tue, 9am–2pm Fri
Kafka's sombre gravemarker lies close to the entrance along Row 21 at the New Jewish Cemetery.

8. Church of the Most Sacred Heart of Our Lord
◉ C6 ⬠ Náměstí Jiřího z Poděbrad, Vinohrady
Designed by famous Slovenian architect Josip Plečnik, this modern building was inspired by old Christian architecture. Its most striking feature is the glass clock in the high tower wall.

9. Villa Müller
◉ Q2 ⬠ Nad Hradním vodojemem 14 ⬡ muzeumprahy.cz/en/visit-villa-muller ✦
An avant-garde masterpiece, this villa by Adolf Loos is a fusion of Functionalism and old English-style design. Reservations needed.

10. DOX Centre for Contemporary Art
◉ S1 ⬠ Poupětova 1, Holešovice
◷ Noon–6pm Wed–Sun ⬡ dox.cz ✦
Set in a former factory, this space presents contemporary international art, architecture and design.

Baroque Břevnov Monastery complex

Vyšehrad Sights

The Romanesque Rotunda of St Martin

1. Sts Peter and Paul Cathedral

📍 Štulcova 🕐 Apr–Oct: 10am–6pm daily (Nov–Mar: to 5pm) ♿

Although the first church to stand on this site was founded by Vratislav II in the 11th century, the Neo-Gothic structure seen today dates back to 1903.

2. Slavín Monument

📍 K Rotundě 🕐 Mar, Apr, Oct: 8am–6pm daily (May–Sep: to 7pm; Nov–Feb: to 5pm)

Set within Vyšehrad Cemetery, this monument marks the burial place of a number of notable Czech cultural figures. Students laid flowers in remembrance here on 17 November 1989, before marching into town for the Velvet Revolution (p11).

3. Devil's Pillar

📍 K Rotundě

The story goes that the devil bet a local priest that he could carry this pillar from the Church of St Mary in Prague to the boundaries of Rome before the clergyman could finish his sermon. Being a sore loser, Satan threw the column he was carrying to the ground here.

4. Tábor Gate (Špička)

📍 V Pevnosti

Charles IV restored Vyšehrad's fortifications in the 14th century.

Catholic crusaders rode through this gate on their way to crush the Táborites in 1434.

5. Congress Centre

This ex-Communist palace of culture now hosts numerous international conferences as well as pop concerts, thanks to its excellent acoustics.

6. Nusle Bridge

This simple, utilitarian viaduct spans the Nusle Valley, connecting Nové Město to the Pankrác banking and commercial district.

7. Cubist Houses

Czech architect Josef Chochol (1880–1956) built several angular masterpieces in the early 20th century. Take the steps down the hill from Vyšehrad Cemetery to visit the impressive buildings at Rašínovo nábřeží 47, Libušina 49 and Neklanova 98.

8. Smetana's Grave

At the start of each year's Prague Spring International Music Festival (p84), musicians attend a ceremony at composer Bedřich Smetana's grave.

9. Casemates

📍 V Pevnosti 46 📞 241 410348 🕐 10am–6pm daily ♿

In the 18th century, occupying French troops drilled niches in Vyšehrad rock and built vaults inside to store arms and ammunition. This now houses six original statues from Charles Bridge (p32).

10. Rotunda of St Martin

📍 K Rotundě

This 11th-century chapel is the oldest in Prague and most likely to be the oldest Christian house of worship in the country. It was reconstructed in 1878.

Cafés and Pubs

Wood-panelled interior of Pastička gastropub

1. Kavárna Pražírna
◘ G6 ⬡ Lublaňská 676/50, Vinohrady
ⓦ kavarnaprazirna.cz
Enjoy the flavour and aroma of freshly roasted Arabica coffees at this café.

2. U Vystřeleného Oka
◘ C6 ⬡ U Božích bojovníků 3, Žižkov
▣ 222 540465 ⏱ Sun
The name "At the Shot-Out Eye" is a tribute to the half-blind Hussite general Jan Žižka from whom Žižkov takes its name and whose enormous statue *(p129)* looms overhead.

3. U Holanů
◘ H7 ⬡ Londýnská 10, Vinohrady
ⓦ uholanu.cz
Tuck into a plate of pickled sausages or herring at Vinohrady's favourite no-nonsense pub. Simple but clean, with perfunctory service.

4. U Houdků
◘ C6 ⬡ Bořivojova 110, Žižkov
ⓦ uhoudku.com
This hidden little gem in Žižkov serves Czech meals that are great value for money. In summer you can sit outside.

5. Palác Akropolis
◘ C6 ⬡ Kubelíkova 27, Žižkov
ⓦ palacakropolis.com
One of the most active independent cultural centres in Prague, Akropolis annually hosts nearly 1,000 cultural events. Both local as well as top international artists perform here.

6. Café Letka
◘ B5 ⬡ Letohradská 44, Bubeneč
ⓦ cafeletka.cz
With its social media-worthy good looks, this café makes a delightful stop at any time of day. Visit for brunch, an afternoon coffee and cake or an evening beer brewed by Matuška, a brewer from Broum.

7. Dva Kohouti
◘ B5 ⬡ Sokolovská 55, Karlín
ⓦ dvakohouti.cz
With dozens of beers on tap, this brewery with a pub is a hugely popular Karlín hangout. Try the exceptional homebrewed pilsner.

8. Čep a pec
◘ G6 ⬡ Svatoplukova 528, Nusle
A friendly, family-run business that prides itself on its authentic and imaginative style. On offer is a wide range of beers and freshly baked goods. Refreshments are made from produce supplied by local farmers.

9. Můj šálek kávy
◘ B5 ⬡ Křižíkova 105, Karlín
ⓦ mujsalekkavy.cz
Sip away at speciality coffee and savour homemade cakes and cookies at the flagship café of Czech double-shot coffee roasters. The interesting decor includes bare walls, books and artworks.

10. Pastička
◘ B6 ⬡ Blanická 25, Vinohrady
ⓦ restaurace-pasticka.cz
The Mousetrap is a perfect blend of old-fashioned beer hall and modish gastropub. Visit it for a choice of light and semi-dark Bernard beer, good, filling food and eclectic Irish decor.

Restaurants

1. Aromi
📍 H5 🏠 Náměstí Míru 6, Prague 2
🌐 aromi.lacollezione.cz · Ⓚ Ⓚ Ⓚ
This Italian restaurant serves up a menu of traditional food accompanied by wines from all around the world.

2. Olympos
📍 C6 🏠 Kubelíkova 9, Žižkov
🌐 tavernaolympos.eu · Ⓚ Ⓚ
Prague's best Greek food is on offer here. The large garden, complete with a children's playground, is ideal for summer dining. The mixed salad platter is the best value around.

3. Mailsi
📍 C6 🏠 Lipanská 1, Žižkov
🌐 mailsi.cz · Ⓚ Ⓚ
This little Pakistani food spot is known for its simple interiors and good-value, flavourful food.

4. SaSaZu
📍 C5 🏠 Bubenské nábřeží 306, Holešovice 🌐 sasazu.com · Ⓚ Ⓚ Ⓚ
This Holešovice landmark offers a menu of exceptional dishes inspired by Asian street food. At night, it also becomes a popular live music venue.

5. Na Kopci
📍 B6 🏠 K Závěrce 20, Praha 5
🌐 nakopci.com · Ⓚ Ⓚ Ⓚ
Featured in the Michelin guide as a "Bib Gourmand" restaurant, Na Kopci offers a four-course degustation menu of French and Czech delicacies created with seasonal and local ingredients.

6. Salabka
📍 B5 🏠 K Bohnicím 2, Praha 7
🕐 Sun–Tue 🌐 salabka.cz · Ⓚ Ⓚ Ⓚ
Surrounded by vast vineyards, this restaurant, located near the district of Troja, is renowned for its award-winning wines. The menu here follows the latest

---

PRICE CATEGORIES
For a three-course meal for one with half a bottle of wine (or equivalent meal), taxes and extra charges
....
Ⓚ under Kč500 Ⓚ Ⓚ Kč500–Kč1,000
Ⓚ Ⓚ Ⓚ over Kč1,000

---

trends with wild game and offers local freshwater fish dishes.

7. Chorvatský Mlýn
📍 A5 🏠 Horoměřichá 3a, Praha 6, Dejvice 🌐 chorvatshymlyn.cz · Ⓚ Ⓚ Ⓚ
Standing on the site of the original 17th-century mill, "Croatian Mill" is located in the centre of the Divoká Šárka Nature Reserve.

8. U Cedru
📍 B5 🏠 Národní Obrany 27, Dejvice
🌐 ucedru.cz · Ⓚ Ⓚ
For a traditional Lebanese dining experience, order pitta with hummus, tabbouleh and other appetizers.

9. ESKA
📍 C6 🏠 Pernerova 49, Karlín
🌐 eska.ambi.cz · Ⓚ Ⓚ
Housed in a former fabric factory, this café, also a bakery and restaurant, serves breakfasts until late afternoon.

10. U Marčanů
📍 A6 🏠 Veleslavínská 14, Prague 6
🌐 umarcanu.cz · Ⓚ
Folk music and dancing make this a fun lunch spot. Large portions of Czech food are served at communal tables. Book ahead and take a taxi.

Aromi's elegant dining room

STREETSMART

One of Prague's trams

GETTING AROUND

Whether exploring Prague by foot or making use of public transport, here is everything you need to know to navigate the city and the areas beyond the centre like a pro.

PUBLIC TRANSPORT COSTS

SHORT TRIP

Kč30

30 mins
including transfers

SINGLE

Kč40

(zones 1-3)

DAY TICKET

Kč120

24 Hours
Unlimited travel

NATIONAL SPEED LIMITS

MOTORWAY

130
km/h
(80 mph)

EXPRESSWAYS

110
km/h
(70 mph)

NATIONAL
ROADS

90
km/h
(60 mph)

URBAN
AREAS

50
km/h
(30 mph)

Arriving by Air

More than 60 international airlines fly to **Václav Havel Airport Prague** (PRG), situated 15 km (9 miles) northwest of the city centre in Ruzyně.

The airport has three terminals. Terminal 1 is used for intercontinental flights to the UK, North America, the Middle East, Africa and Asia. All domestic flights and flights to destinations within the EU and other Schengen countries are served by Terminal 2. These two terminals are connected and are only a short walk apart. Terminal 3, is used for general aviation and private planes.

Getting to and from Prague airport is easy, relatively fast and economical. Allow at least 60 minutes to reach the airport by road from the city centre at rush hour. Travelling by a combination of the metro and standard bus takes about 45 minutes depending on connections. There is a shared shuttle bus run by **Prague Airport Shuttles** that goes to the city centre every 15 minutes. You can also request to be dropped off at your accommodation. For information on journey times and ticket prices, see the table below.

Václav Havel Airport Prague
W prg.aero
Prague Airport Shuttles
W prague-airport-shuttle.cz

International Train Travel

Regular high-speed international trains connect Prague's Hlavní nádraží and Nádraží Holešovice stations to major cities in Europe. Reservations for these services are essential as seats book up, particularly in the busy summer months.

You can buy tickets and passes for multiple international journeys from **Eurail** or **Interrail**, however you may still need to pay an additional reservation fee depending on what rail service you travel with. Always check that your pass is valid before boarding. Students and those under the age of 26 can benefit from discounted rail travel.

Eurail
w eurail.com
Interrail
w interrail.eu

Domestic Train Travel

The railways in the Czech Republic are run by České Dráhy (**ČD**).

The biggest and busiest railway station in Prague is Hlavní nádraží, which is only a five-minute walk from Wenceslas Square. After a thorough renovation, the Art Nouveau station now features a gleaming interior with shops, restaurants, a pub and even a jeweller. The lower ground floor has an inexpensive left-luggage facility and the central ticket office (open 3:20am –12:30am). There is also a ČD Travel office, where all international rail tickets are available from multilingual station staff and ticket machines.

There are several types of train services operating in Prague and throughout the Czech Republic, including the *rychlík* (express) trains, which are used for longer distances; and the *osobní* (passenger) trains which form a local service and stop at all stations.

Tickets can be bought in advance. If you want to buy a ticket just before your train leaves, be aware that queues at ticket booths can be long.

On the timetable, an "R" in a box by a train number means you must have a seat reserved on that train. An "R" without a box means a reservation is recommended. If you are caught in the wrong carriage, you will have to pay an on-the-spot fine.
ČD
w cd.cz

Public Transport

Prague's bus, tram and metro services are provided by the Prague Public Transport Company (**DPP**). Its website and app provide timetables, ticket information, transport maps and more.

The best way of getting around Prague by public transport is by tram or metro. Prague's rush hours are between 6am and 9am and 3pm and 5pm, Monday to Friday. However, more trains, trams and buses run at these times, so crowding is not usually a problem. Some bus routes to the suburbs only run during peak hours.
DPP
w dpp.cz

Tickets

Prague has a fully integrated public transport system and tickets are valid on most forms of public transport. A separate ticket is needed for the funicular railway that runs from Újezd to the top of Petřín Hill.

Tickets are available from machines at metro stations, main tram stops and at most news stands (*tabák*).

Buy tickets before you travel and validate them in the machines provided. Periodic checks are carried out by ticket inspectors who will levy an on-the-spot fine if you are caught without a valid ticket. Those under six and over 70 travel free and tickets for people aged 6–15 and 60–65 years are half price (any form of ID card or passport is accepted).

Individual ticket prices add up; longer-term tickets are good value if you are planning on exploring the city thoroughly. Network tickets offer unlimited travel for for one day (Kč120) and three days (Kč330).

GETTING TO AND FROM THE AIRPORT

Transport	Journey time	Price
Airport Express Bus	35–50 mins	Kč60
Metro/Bus/Night Bus	45–50 mins	Kč32
Shuttle Bus	30 mins–1hr	Kč290
Taxi	30 mins–1hr	Kč600

Buses

Visitors are likely to use a bus only to travel to and from the airport, or to sights further out of town. There are three bus lines that operate in Malá Strana, Staré Město and Nové Město.

Bus timetables are located at every stop. Daytime buses run from 5am to midnight every 6–30 minutes. Night buses (routes 901–915) operate from midnight to 4:30am and run every 20–60 minutes.

Validate your pre-bought tickets in the machine located at each door.

Long-Distance Bus Travel

Long-distance bus or coach travel can be a cheap option for those visiting Prague. Some Czech towns, such as Karlovy Vary, Hradec Králové, Český Krumlov and Terezín, are much easier to reach by coach than train.

The city's main bus terminal is Florenc, on the northeastern edge of the Nové Město.

Flixbus and **RegioJet** offer a variety of routes to Prague from other European cities as well as several domestic routes.

Flixbus
🆆 flixbus.com
RegioJet
🆆 regiojet.com

Trams

Prague's most efficient method of public transport is the city's comprehensive tram network, which covers a large area, including the city centre.

Maps and timetables at tram stops help you locate your destination and route. On the timetable, the stop you are at will be underlined and the direction of travel is given by the terminus station.

Routes 6, 9, 17 and 22 are the most useful for getting around the centre of Prague. They pass many of the major sights on both sides of the Vltava, and are a pleasant way of sightseeing.

Trams run 4:30am–12:30am daily. Night trams (routes 91–99) run every 30 minutes and are marked by white numbers on a dark background at stops.

Metro

The metro is the fastest way to get around the city. Prague's underground system has four lines (A, B, C and D) operating from 5am until midnight.

Line A (green) is the most useful line for tourists, covering all the main areas of the city centre including the shopping area around Wenceslas Square.

Stations are signposted in both English and Czech, and feature information panels in a number of languages.

Prague by Boat

Boat tours along the Vltava river offer fabulous views of Prague's major sights. Most run during the summer months, and include tours, romantic dinner cruises and private rentals.

Tickets can be booked in advance from tour providers. Check out **Evropská Vodní Doprava** or **Prague Boats**. Alternatively you can enquire on the day at the boarding points along the river.

Prague Boats
🆆 prague-boats.cz
Evropská Vodní Doprava
🆆 evd.cz

Taxis

All taxis in Prague are privately owned, and there are many unscrupulous drivers who are out to charge as much as they can get away with. If you think you have been scammed by a taxi driver, take their name and number so you can report them to the police.

Look for Fair Place taxi ranks marked with a yellow "taxi" sign and an orange "thumbs up" icon. Taxis that stop here will guarantee the maximum charges of Kč40 boarding fee, Kč36 per km travel and Kč6 per minute waiting. After the journey, the driver is obliged to print an official receipt.

Taxi companies that are safe to hail on the street include **AAA Taxi**. However, the cheapest way to get a taxi is to phone or use the company's mobile app.

AAA Taxi
🆆 aaataxi.cz

Driving

Driving in Prague is not recommended. The city's complex web of one-way streets, lack of parking and pedestrianized areas make driving very difficult.

Driving to Prague

The Czech Republic is easily reached by car from most countries in Europe via E-roads, the International European Road Network.

Prague is connected to every major border crossing by motorways (D roads. To drive on the motorway you will need to display a special highway toll sticker available at the border, petrol stations and post offices.

Driving in Prague

Driving in Prague can be stressful and should be avoided. If you do drive, beware of cyclists and trams. Trams take precedence; take care when turning; and allow cyclists priority.

Vehicles must be parked on the right-hand side of the road, with the exception of one-way streets. Parking spaces in the centre are scarce, and the penalties for illegal parking are harsh. **Parkuj v klidu** provide detailed information regarding parking. Meter parking from 8am to 8pm costs a maximum Kč80 per hour and varies in price and length between orange, blue and violet zones. Unfortunately, car theft in Prague is rife. Try to park in an official – preferably underground – car park or at one of the guarded car parks (look for the "P+R" symbol) at the edge of the city and use public transport to travel into the centre.

If a car accident occurs, the vehicle cannot be moved until there has been a police inspection of the site. In case of emergency, you can call the road traffic assistance, Autoklub Bohemia Assistance (**ÚAMK**), by dialling the phone number 1240.

Parkuj v klidu
🔳 parkujvklidu.cz
ÚAMK
🔳 uamk.cz

Car Rental

To rent a car in the Czech Republic, you must be at least 21 years old and have held a valid licence for at least one year. Drivers under the age of 26 may incur a young driver surcharge.

Rules of the Road

Always drive on the right. Unless signposted otherwise, vehicles coming from the right have right of way.

At all times, drivers must carry a valid driver's licence, registration and insurance documents.

The law states that all occupants should wear seat belts. Small children must travel in the back seat and the use of a mobile phone while driving is strictly prohibited, with the exception of a hands-free system.

Cycling

Prague is generally a bike-friendly city, with many cycle lanes. Bicycles can be rented hourly or by the day. Deposits are usually paid upfront and refunded on return. **Praha Bike** offers private rentals and tours while public bicycle schemes such as **Rekola**, operated through an app, are also available.

Ride on the right. Beware of tram tracks; cross them at an angle to avoid getting stuck. For your own safety, do not walk with your bike in a bike lane or cycle in pedestrian zones, or in the dark without lights. Wearing a helmet is recommended.

Praha Bike
🔳 prahabike.cz
Rekola
🔳 rekola.cz

Walking

The city centre is compact and walking is the best way to see the city. Wear flat-soled comfortable shoes, watch your step on the cobblestones and be aware that trams have priority.

Guided walking tours abound, with themes that include historic Prague and haunted Prague. Most meet below the Astronomical Clock in Old Town Square.

PRACTICAL INFORMATION

A little local know-how goes a long way in Prague. On these pages you can find all the essential advice and information you will need to make the most of your trip to this city.

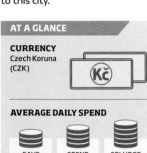

AT A GLANCE

CURRENCY
Czech Koruna
(CZK)

AVERAGE DAILY SPEND

SAVE	SPEND	SPLURGE
Kč2500	Kč4000	Kč5000+

BOTTLED WATER	COFFEE	BEER	DINNER FOR TWO
Kč25	Kč65	Kč45	Kč1,250

ESSENTIAL PHRASES

Hello	Dobrý den
Goodbye	Na shledanou
Please	Prosím
Thank you	Děkuji vám
Do you speak English?	Mluvíte anglicky?
I don't understand...	Nerozumím

ELECTRICITY SUPPLY

Power sockets are type E, fitting two-pronged plugs. Standard voltage is 230 volts.

Passports and Visas

For entry requirements, including visas, consult your nearest Czech embassy or check the **Ministry of Foreign Affairs of the Czech Republic** website. Citizens of the UK, US, Canada, Australia and New Zealand do not need a visa for stays of up to three months, but must apply in advance for the European Travel Information and Authorization System (**ETIAS**); roll-out has continually been postponed so check website for details. Visitors from other countries may also require an ETIAS, so check before travelling. EU nationals do not need a visa or an ETIAS.
ETIAS
W etiasvisa.com
Ministry of Foreign Affairs of the Czech Republic
W mzv.cz

Government Advice

It is important to seek both your and the Czech government's advice before travelling. The **UK Foreign, Commonwealth & Development Office (FCDO)**, the **US State Department**, the **Australian Department of Foreign Affairs and Trade** and the Ministry of Foreign Affairs of the Czech Republic offer the latest information on security, health and local laws.
Australian Department of Foreign Affairs and Trade
W smartraveller.gov.au
FCDO
W gov.uk/foreign-travel-advice
US State Department
W travel.state.gov

Customs Information

You can find information on the laws relating to goods and currency taken in or out of the Czech Republic on the **Customs Administration of the Czech Republic** website.
Customs Administration of the Czech Republic
W celnisprava.cz

Insurance

We recommend taking out a comprehensive insurance policy covering theft, loss of belongings, medical care, cancellations and delays, and read the small print carefully. The Czech Republic has reciprocal health agreements with other EU countries. EU and UK citizens are eligible for free emergency treatment provided they have a valid European Health Insurance Card (EHIC) or UK Global Health Insurance Card (**GHIC**).

GHIC
ⓦ ghic.org.uk

Vaccinations

No vaccinations are necessary.

Money

Most establishments accept major credit, debit and prepaid currency cards. Contactless payments are becoming increasingly common, but it's always a good idea to carry some cash for smaller items and local markets.

Tipping in restaurants (around 10 per cent) is considered polite – though overzealous tipping can cause embarrassment. In hotels, porters generally expect Kč50 per bag, housekeeping Kč30 per day and the concierge Kč30–50 per day. Taxi drivers don't expect a tip.

Travellers with Specific Requirements

Narrow streets and uneven paving make Prague difficult for wheelchair users. However, services are improving. Most public buildings are now fitted with entry ramps.

Most of the trams and buses have low access, and the majority of metro stations are fitted with lifts. Timetables at tram stops indicate which services are wheelchair-accessible. Visit the Prague Public Transport Company (**DPP**) website to plan your journey using wheelchair-accessible metro stations, trams and buses.

Airport assistance is available for free but must be booked in advance

through your airline or travel agency. **Accessible Prague** can arrange transport from the airport to the city centre for wheelchair users. They can also help with finding suitable accommodation and they organize tours and day trips tailored to visitors' needs.

The **Prague Organization of Wheelchair Users** has a range of resources available, including interactive maps and guides in Braille.

Accessible Prague
ⓦ accessibleprague.com
Prague Organization of Wheelchair Users
ⓦ presbariery.cz
Prague Public Transport Company
ⓦ dpp.cz/en/barrier-free-travel

Language

Czech is the official language of the Czech Republic. Those working in the tourist industry usually have a good level of English, but it's appreciated if you know a few phrases in Czech.

Opening Hours

Shops in the city centre generally open from 9am to 6pm Monday to Saturday. Malls and shopping centres stay open until 8pm or 9pm. Some shops close early on Saturdays and close for the day on Sundays. Public transport also runs a reduced service at weekends.

Various museums and attractions are closed on Mondays. Last admission to many attractions is 30 minutes before closing.

On public holidays, schools, banks and most public services are closed and some museums, attractions and shops are closed while others will close early.

Situations can change quickly and unexpectedly. Always check before visiting attractions and hospitality venues for up-to-date opening hours and booking requirements.

Personal Security

Prague is relatively safe and violence is rare. Pickpocketing is common, particularly on crowded trams and the metro, and at popular tourist sites. Use your common sense and be alert to your surroundings. Avoid hailing taxis on the street; instead, call or ask someone to call a reliable radio taxi *(p138)*.

AT A GLANCE

EMERGENCY NUMBERS

GENERAL EMERGENCY

112

POLICE

158

AMBULANCE

155

FIRE SERVICE

150

TIME ZONE
CET/CEST: Central European Summer Time runs from the last Sunday in March to the last Sunday in October.

TAP WATER
Unless stated otherwise, tap water in Prague is safe to drink.

WEBSITES AND APPS

prague.eu
Prague City Tourism - Prague's official tourist information website

DPP Prague Public Transport
Prague's official public transport website (dpp.cz) and app

Lítačka
Buy paperless public transport tickets direct from your mobile or smart device

Pivní Deníček
An app showing the nearest bar to your location, which beer they serve on tap and how much it costs

---

If you have anything stolen, report the crime as soon as possible to the nearest police station, and bring ID with you. Get a copy of the crime report in order to claim on your insurance.

If you have your passport stolen, or if you are involved in a serious crime or accident, contact your embassy as soon as possible.

Generally, Czechs are accepting of all people, regardless of their race, gender or sexuality. Prague has an active LGBTQ+ scene with many venues for the community and an annual Pride event, held each August. Homosexuality was legalized in 1962 but same-sex marriages aren't recognized in Czech law. If you do feel unsafe, the **Safe Space Alliance** pinpoints your nearest place of refuge.

Safe Space Alliance
W safespacealliance.com

Health

The Czech Republic has a world-class healthcare system. Emergency medical care is free for all UK and EU citizens. If you have an EHIC or GHIC *(p141)*, be sure to present this as soon as possible.

For other visitors, payment of hopsital bills and medical expenses is the patient's responsibility. As such it is important to arrange comprehensive medical insurance beforehand. You may still have to pay upfront for medical treatment and reclaim later.

For minor ailments and prescriptions go to a pharmacy *(lékárna)*. These are easily identified by a large green cross. Details of the nearest 24-hour service are usually displayed in windows.

Smoking, Alcohol and Drugs

Prague has a strict smoking ban in all public spaces including buildings, bars, cafés, shops, restaurants and hotels.

The possession of narcotics is limited. Possession of illegal substances could result in prosecution and a possible prison sentence.

There is no blanket ban on the consumption of alcohol on the streets;

however, drinking alcohol on the bus or train and in metro stations, parks, playgrounds and near schools is banned and may incur a fine. Many Staré Město streets have banned walking around with an open bottle or can.

The Czech Republic enforces a strict zero tolerance policy on drink-driving. This also applies to cyclists.

ID

It is compulsory for visitors to carry a form of ID at all times, or failing that, a photocopy of your passport.

Responsible Tourism

As one of Europe's most-visited cities, Prague suffers from overtourism and inebriated visitors are a real problem. Do your bit to support the city by being considerate to locals, particularly in residential areas (making loud noises in some areas can incur a fine).

Returnable cups are common in markets and at events, so make use of them and avoid single-use plastics. Dropping litter on the streets and in parks comes with a hefty on-the-spot fine, so use publicly available bins or take your litter with you.

Buying local goes a long way; avoid tourist traps and seek out locally owned retailers and crafters.

Visiting Places of Worship

Dress respectfully; talk quietly and avoid using flash photography. When visiting synagogues, cover your head and never turn your back on the ark.

Mobile Phones and Wi-Fi

Free Wi-Fi hotspots are widely available in Prague's city centre. Cafés and restaurants usually permit the use of their Wi-Fi on the condition that you make a purchase. Visitors travelling to Prague with EU tariffs can use their devices abroad without being affected by data roaming charges. Users will be charged the same rates for data, SMS and voice calls as they would pay at home.

Postal Services

Stamps can be bought from post offices, newsagents and tobacconists (tabák).

Parcels and registered letters must be sent from a post office. There is no first- or second-class mail, but the majority of letters usually arrive at their destination within a few days.

Taxes and Refunds

VAT in the Czech Republic is usually around 20 per cent for most items. Non-EU residents are entitled to a tax refund on single purchases exceeding Kč2000, subject to certain conditions. This does not include tobacco or alcohol.

When you make a purchase, ask the sales assistant for a tax-free cheque. When leaving the country, present this form, along with the goods receipt and your ID at customs.

Discount Cards

There are a number of passes or cards available to tourists visiting the city.

One such card is the **Prague Cool Pass**, which provides free entry to over 70 attractions and discounted entry to many more, as well as discounted tours, cruises and concerts. Passes are valid for one to ten days (from €55 to €139) and are available as a digital pass via a mobile app or as a physical card.

Free or discounted entry to Prague's most popular tours and attractions is included with **Prague City Pass**. The card costs Kč1390 and is valid for 30 days from first use. Available online and from participating tourist offices.

The **Prague Visitor Pass** includes entry to almost 70 attractions, discounts on tours, events and more, plus free travel on public transport. The card is valid for 48, 72 or 120 hours from first use and is available online and from some official Prague tourist offices.

Prague City Pass
🅦 praguecitypass.com
Prague CoolPass
🅦 praguecoolpass.com
Prague Visitor Pass
🅦 praguevisitorpass.eu

PLACES TO STAY

From opulent Art Nouveau hotels to cosy family-run inns, Prague has a hotel to suit every type of traveller. Seeking a luxurious stay? Bed down in a former palace. All about location? Choose a hotel next to the Charles Bridge or Old Town Square. Want to be in the thick of the nightlife scene? Go for a hostel in Greater Prague.

Historic hotels are everywhere, but take the chance to explore the city's quirkier side too, perhaps staying on a moored boat along the river or a retro spot with Pop Art flourishes.

PRICE CATEGORIES

For a standard, double room per night (with breakfast if included), taxes and extra charges.

Kč under Kč3,000
Kč Kč Kč3,000–6,000
Kč Kč Kč over Kč6,000

Staré Město

Ahoy! Hostel

L6 ⌂ Na Perštýně 10
ahoyhostel.com · Kč

It's hard to find an excellent, low-cost option in Staré Město, but that's where Ahoy! comes in. With those pennies you've saved you can treat yourself to a cheap Czech beer from the hostel's fridge or explore the Old Town Square, just a five-minute walk away. Or, keep costs down even further at the hostel's free evening events.

Aurus Hotel

K4 ⌂ Karlova 3
adrezliving.com · Kč Kč

If you're seeking a peaceful getaway but still want to be in the thick of the action, book into the family-run Aurus Hotel. Though situated on the historic Royal Route, just minutes away from Charles Bridge and the Old Town Square, the UNESCO-listed building sits on the quietest street in the area. Inside, it's an old-world sanctuary, with rooms complemented by high-beamed ceilings, wooden fittings and antique furnishings.

Hotel Josef

N2 ⌂ Rybná 20
hoteljosef.com · Kč Kč

Hoping to keep up your fitness regime on holiday? Hotel Josef will keep you on track. Not only is this modern, minimalist hotel home to a superb rooftop gym, it also hosts free organized runs every Tuesday and Friday morning. Get your sweat on then enjoy a smoothie and freshly baked goods from the onsite French bakery.

Buddha-Bar Hotel

N3 ⌂ Jakubská 649/8
buddhabarhotel
prague.com · Kč Kč

With its dragon murals, decadent red-and-gold colour scheme and a 3-ft (1-m) Buddha in the lobby, this luxury hotel is a slice of east Asia in central Europe. The theme extends to the amenities, too; the restaurant serves delicious pan-Asian dishes, and the spa offers signature rituals like the so-called "Journey to Bali".

The Emblem Hotel

L3 ⌂ Platnéřshá 19
emblemprague.com
· Kč Kč Kč

This five-star hotel is adored for many reasons: an excellent spa, a stunning collection of contemporary art and various chill-out spaces where both locals and visitors can lounge, drink or work. Above all, though, it's the George Prime Steak – one of the city's best steak restaurants – that people shout about the most; try the T-bone.

Hotel Paříž

P3 ⌂ U Obecního domu
1 hotel-paris.cz · Kč Kč Kč

With its vaulted ceilings, golden statues and grand lobby staircase, this hotel is a time capsule of early 20th-century Art Nouveau elegance. A complimentary drink at check-in is the cherry on top.

The Mozart

📍 K5 🏠 Karolíny Světlé 34
🌐 themozart.com · Kč Kč Kč

It's said that Count Jan Pachta, who owned this former palace, jokingly locked Mozart in one of the rooms here until he composed a piece for Pachta's orchestra. True or not, Mozart did indeed stay here in his heyday. Follow suit and you're promised a beautiful riverside location, sumptuous rooms and romantic courtyards that host summer concerts.

Malá Strana

Vintage Design Hotel Sax

📍 B3 🏠 Jánský vršeh 3
🌐 sax.cz · Kč Kč

This retro hotel is worlds away from its neighbouring medieval monuments, and therein lies its unique charm. All rooms are decorated in styles that reflect the 50s, 60s and 70s, like abstract wallpaper and Pop Art touches, and decked out with original period furniture. It's a short walk to the Lennon Wall, should you desire more bohemian vibes.

Hotel Pod Věží

📍 D3 🏠 Mostecká 2
🌐 podvezi.com · Kč Kč

There's a novelty to staying right by the tower at Charles Bridge, but that's not all this hotel has going for it. Its creperie is the icing on the cake (or the topping on the crepe), serving up sweet and savoury crepes as well as fresh sandwiches and salads.

Golden Well Hotel

📍 C2 🏠 U Zlaté studně 4
🌐 goldenwell.cz · Kč Kč Kč

This place is worth a stay for the breakfast on the rooftop terrace alone. Luckily, there's plenty more to keep you happy here, starting with its romantic location in a 16th-century regal residence, set beside the adjoining Ledeburg Gardens. Better yet, rooms feature whirlpool baths and stunning Richelieu furniture.

Charles Bridge Hostel

📍 D3 🏠 Mostecká 4
🌐 charlesbridgehostel.com · Kč

As its name suggests, this hostel is all about location, location, location. Close to the Charles Bridge, it's a budget-friendly option in a fairly expensive part of the city, and your money goes even further here with the free tours, guidebook rentals and discounts on several experiences in Prague.

The Augustine

📍 D2 🏠 Letenská 12/33
🌐 marriott.com · Kč Kč Kč

It might be part of the Marriott's "Luxury Collection" today, but this former 13th-century monastery hasn't forgotten its roots. Vaulted ceilings, original doors and exposed beams are a reminder of the complex's past life, and former monks' quarters have been transformed into beautiful rooms with decor inspired by 20th-century Czech Cubism. Oh, and the monastery still brews its own beer according to an Augustinian monastic recipe; enjoy a pint in the hotel's restaurant.

Prague Castle and Hradčany

Questenberg Hotel

📍 A3 🏠 Úvoz 15/155
🌐 questenberg.cz · Kč Kč

Views, glorious views! Stay at this small Baroque hotel and you'll be treated to stunning vistas over Prague, from the Petřín Gardens down to Malá Strana and Staré Město. The price to pay for such a treat is a relatively long uphill walk from Malá Strana, but trust us when we say it's worth it.

Romantický Hotel U Raka

📍 A2 🏠 Černínská 10
🌐 hoteluraka.cz · Kč Kč

Everything about this family-run place feels suitably homely. On a quiet street near Prague Castle, 18th-century timber walls encase cosy, country-style rooms dotted with antique furnishings. When making a reservation, book room No 6, which has its own private garden and a fireplace. This is truly a lovely place to be.

Hotel Savoy
📍A2 🏠Keplerova 6
🌐savoyprague.cz · Kč Kč

What do Tina Turner, David Bowie and the Spice Girls have in common? Aside from their singing chops, they've all bedded down at this grand hotel, a former 19th-century cinema that retains its star quality today. The Art Nouveau building exudes historic glamour, with a marble-floored lobby, vintage furniture in the common areas and rooms decked out with traditional wooden furnishings and patterned carpets.

Josefov and Northern Staré Město
....

Residence Bene
📍N2 🏠Dlouhá 48
🌐residence-bene.cz · Kč

Locations rarely get much better than this, let alone at this price. Book a stay here and you're just minutes from the best sites in both Josefov and Staré Město, including a quick hop, skip and jump to the Old Town Square. The rooms are no-frills, but you'll hardly be spending much time inside.

River Hotel Königstein
📍L1 🏠Königstein, Dvořáhovo nábřeží
🌐riverhotel.cz · Kč Kč

Even better than taking a boat tour along the Vltava river? Letting its gentle waters lull you to sleep. This place offers something completely different from the rest of the city – the chance to stay on a moored boat on the river's banks. And when you wake, step onto the upper deck for breakfast with views of Prague Castle.

The President
📍L1 🏠Náměstí Curieových 1 🌐axxos hotels.com · Kč Kč

The Brutalist exterior of this former communist building couldn't be more different from its slick modern interior. Rooms are kitted out with designer furniture, beautiful artworks and huge windows that let in ample light – perfect for looking out across the river over to Prague Castle. Best of all, the excellent Elements restaurant serves top Czech and global cuisine.

Nové Město
....

MeetMe23
📍G4 🏠Washingtonova 23 🌐meetme23.com · Kč

Forever losing your room key? MeetMe23 has got your back; you unlock your room with your phone here, and that's just the start of how this hotel embraces tech. A virtual receptionist greets you when you arrive, a "virtual flight" video over Prague inspires your itinerary and there's even a 3D printer where you can print out a souvenir of the so-called "Blueman", a blue figure you'll see around the hotel. It's wacky, forward-thinking and, ironically, housed in a historic building.

The ICON
📍F4 🏠V jámě 6
🌐iconhotel.eu · Kč Kč

The ICON is proof that luxury can be found at a reasonable price. Rooms include high-end amenities you'd expect from truly luxurious places, including high thread-count bed linens that cover natural, handmade Swedish beds and complimentary Rituals toiletries. An excellent tapas restaurant and all-day breakfast top it off.

Mosaic House Design Hotel
📍E5 🏠Odboru 4
🌐mosaichouse.com · Kč Kč

Mosaic isn't just about offering you the best stay (but that it does, with cosy rooms, a stylish café and private spa). It's also committed to offering a sustainable stay. Not only was this the first hotel in the Czech Republic to reuse and recycle waste water, it was also the country's first CO_2-neutral hotel, and even makes its own soil. A beautiful garden oasis seals the deal.

NYX Hotel Prague
📍P5 🏠Panshá 9 🌐nyx-hotels.com/prague · Kč Kč

If you want to feel like you're staying in a work of art, book into NYX.

This design-led hotel was originally designed by the famous Modernist architect Josef Gočar, and it's filled with street art by local artists that lend the space a sense of urban chic. Things gets even cooler at the 360° Lounge Bar, where signature cocktails are served to live music.

Hotel NH Collection Prague Carlo IV

📍 H3 🏠 Senovážné náměstí 13 🌐 dahotels. com · Kč Kč Kč

This hotel might be set in a former 19th-century palace, but it wasn't royalty who spent time here; rather, the building was a former bank, and you get what you pay for at this sophisticated spot. Choose a room in the "historical wing", filled with beautifully designed Italian furniture, and lean into the opulence at the bar, set in an old bank vault.

Miss Sophie's New Town

📍 G6 🏠 Melounova 3 🌐 miss-sophies.com · Kč

What makes this place so loved? It could be the spa, where you can relax in a hot tub, sweat it out in an infrared sauna and snack on nuts and fruit in between. Or maybe it's the buffet breakfast, a top display of meats, cheeses, omelettes and pancakes. Whatever it is, Miss Sophie's is the perfect retreat from the bustle of the city.

The Grand Mark

📍 G3 🏠 Hybernská 12 🌐 grandmark.cz · Kč Kč Kč

Nestled in a former Baroque palace, the Grand Mark is still fit for royalty today. Rooms are elegantly furnished, the Le Grill Restaurant serves up beautifully plated dishes beneath a grand chandelier, and a private courtyard garden is the ideal place to pass a peaceful evening.

Greater Prague

Czech Inn

📍 R2 🏠 Francouzshá 76, Vršovice 🌐 czech-inn. com · Kč

You're going to want to check in to this hostel – it could well be Prague's most sociable. Live music, DJs, movie nights and quizzes are just some of the events that keep guests entertained at night, all of which are the perfect way to meet people to explore the popular bars along nearby Krymská with.

Brix Hostel

📍 S2 🏠 Roháčova 15, Žižhov 🌐 brixhostel. com · Kč

You'll be hard-pressed to find somewhere more ideally located for Žižkov's vibrant nightlife scene. With a large communal terrace and multi-bed dorms (including all-female options), Brix is perfect for meeting likeminded night owls to hit the town with. And, if you're lucky, a stay at Brix might even coincide with one of the hostel's impromptu party nights.

Mama Shelter

📍 R1 🏠 Veletržní 1502/20, Holešovice 🌐 mama shelter.com/prague · Kč Kč

The local branch of a trendy global chain, Mama Shelter is popular for good reason. An epic terrace for casual drinks? Check. A legendary Sunday brunch? Correct. Pool tables and table football? Naturally. Add to that DJ nights and you've got a hotel you'll struggle to leave.

Botanique Hotel

📍 R2 🏠 Sokolovská 11, Karlín 🌐 hotelbotanique. com · Kč Kč

The Botanique means business when it comes to eco-friendly practices. Recyclable Nespresso capsules feature in every room, keys are wooden (not plastic) and vegan and vegetarian menus are offered (online, to save paper). Even better, you can charge your electric car here for free.

Hotel Le Palais

📍 R2 🏠 U Zvonařhy 1, Vinohrady 🌐 lepalais hotel.eu · Kč Kč Kč

If you're looking for a plush belle époque villa stay in one of Prague's most desirable neigh-bourhoods, Le Palais is for you. You'll have access to your own reading room, a spa and wellness centre. Step outside for the gorgeous Havlíčkovy sady park.

INDEX

PHRASE BOOK

In an Emergency

Help!	Pomoc!	po-mots
Stop!	Zastavte!	zas-tav-te
Call a doctor!	Zavolejte doktora!	za-vo-ley-te dok-to-ra!
Call an ambulance!	Zavolejte sanitku!	za-vo-ley-te sa-nit-ku!
Call the police!	Zavolejte policii!	za-vo-ley-te poli-tsi-yi!
Call the fire brigade!	Zavolejte hasiče	za-vo-ley-te ha-si-che
Where is the telephone?	Kde je telefon?	gde ye te-le-fohn?
the nearest hospital?	nejbližší nemocnice?	ney-blizh-shee ne-mo-tsnyi-tse?

Communication Essentials

Yes/No	Ano/Ne	ano/ne
Please	Prosím	pro-seem
Thank you	Děkuji vám	dye-ku-ji vahm
Excuse me	Prosím vás	pro-seem vahs
Hello	Dobrý den	do-bree den
Goodbye	Na shledanou	na shle-da-nou
Good evening	Dobrý večer	do-bree ve-cher
morning	ráno	rah-no
afternoon	odpoledne	od-po-led-ne
evening	večer	ve-cher
yesterday	včera	vche-ra
today	dnes	dnes
tomorrow	zítra	zee-tra
here	tady	ta-di
there	tam	tam
What?	Co?	tso?
When?	Kdy?	gdi?
Why?	Proč?	proch?
Where?	Kde?	gde?

Useful Phrases

How are you?	Jak se máte?	yak se mah-te?
Very well, thank you.	Velmi dobře děkuji	vel-mi do-brze dye-ku-yi
Pleased to meet you	Těší mě	tye-shee mnye
See you soon	Uvidíme se brzy	u-vi-dyee-me-se brzy
That's fine	To je v pořádku	to ye vpo-rzhahdku
Where is/are…?	Kde je/jsou …?	gde ye/ysou …?
How long does it take to get to…?	Jak dlouho to trvá se dostat do…?	yak dlou-ho to tr-vah se dos-tat …?
How do I get to…?	Jak se dostanu k …?	yak se dos-ta-nuh k …?
Do you speak English?	Mluvíte anglicky?	mlu-vee-te an-glits-ki?
I don't understand	Nerozumím	ne-ro-zu-meem
Could you speak more slowly?	Mohl(a)* byste mluvit trochu pomaleji?	mo-hl(a) bys-te mlu-vit tro-khu po-ma-ley?
Pardon?	Prosím?	pro-seem?
I'm lost	Ztratil(a)* jsem se	stra-tyil (a) ysem se

Sightseeing

art gallery	galerie	ga-le-ri-ye
bus stop	autobusová zastávka	au-to-bus-o-vah za-stah-vka
church	kostel	kos-tel
garden	zahrada	za-hra-da
library	knihovna	knyi-hov-na
museum	muzeum	mu-ze-um
railway station	nádraží	nah-dra-zhee
tourist information	turistické informace	tu-ris-tits-ke in-for-ma-tse
closed for the public holiday	státní svátek	staht-nyee svah-tek

Shopping

How much does it cost?	Co to stojí?	tso to sto-yee?
I would like…	Chtěl(a)* bych…	khtyel(a) bikh…
Do you have…?	Máte…?	maa-te …?
I'm just looking	Jenom se dívám	ye-nom se dyee-vahm
Do you take credit cards?	Berete kreditní karty?	be-re-te kre-dit –nyee kar-ti?
What time do you open/ close?	V kolik otevíráte/ zavíráte?	v ko-lik o-te-vee-rah-te/ za-vee-rah-te?
this one	tento	ten-to
that one	tamten	tam-ten
expensive	drahý	dra-hee
cheap	levný	lev-nee
size	velikost	ve-li-kost
white	bílý	bee-lee
black	černý	cher-nee
red	červený	cher-ve-nee
yellow	žlutý	zhlu-tee
green	zelený	ze-le-nee
blue	modrý	mod-ree
brown	hnědý	hnye-dee

Types of Shop

antique shop	starožitnictví	sta-ro zhit--
bank	banka	ban-ka
bakery	pekárna	pe-kahr-na
bookstore	knihkupectví	knih-kupets-tvee
butcher	řeznictví	rzhez-nyits-tvee
chemist (pre-scriptions etc)	lékárna	leh-kahr-na
chemist (toiletries etc)	drogerie	dro-ge-riye
delicatessen	lahůdky	la-hood-ki
department store	obchodní dům	op-khod-nyee doom
grocery	potraviny	po-tra-vi-ni
glass	sklo	sklo
market	trh	trh
post office	pošta	posh-ta
supermarket	samoobsluha	sa-mo-ob-slu-ha
tobacconist	tabák	ta-bahk
travel agency	cestovní kancelář	tses-tov-nyi kan-tse-laarzh

Staying in a Hotel

Do you have a vacant room?	Máte volný pokoj?	mah-te vol-nee po-koy?
double room	dvoulůžkový pokoj	dvou-loozh-ko-vee po-koy

with double bed	s dvojitou postelí	s dvoy-tou pos-te-lee
twin room	pokoj s dvěma postelemi	po-koy sdvye-ma pos-te-le-mi
porter	vrátný	vrah-tnee
key	klíč	kleech l
have a reservation	Mám reservaci	mahm re-zer-va-tsi

Eating Out

Have you got a table for…?	Máte stůl pro …?	mah-te stool pro …?
I'd like to reserve a table	Chtěl(a)* bych rezervovat stůl	khtyel(a) bikh re-zer-vo-vat stool
breakfast	snídaně	snyee-danye
lunch	oběd	ob-yed
dinner	večeře	ve-che-rzhe
The bill, please	Prosím, účet	pro-seem oo-chet
I am a vegetarian	Jsem vegetarián (ka)*	ysem veghe-tariahn(ka)
waitress!	slečno	slech-no
waiter!	pane vrchní!	pane vrkh-nyee!
fixed-price menu	standardní menu	stan-dard-nyee menu
dish of the day	nabídka dne	na-beed-ka dne
starter	předkrm	przhed-krm
main course	hlavní jídlo	hlav-nyee yeed-lo
vegetables	zelenina	ze-le-nyi-na
dessert	zákusek	zah-kusek
cover charge	poplatek	pop-la-tek
wine list	nápojový lístek	nah-po-yo-vee lees-tek
rare (steak)	krvavý	kr-va-vee
medium	středně udělaný	strzhed-nye u-dye-la-nee
well done	dobře udělaný	dobrzhe- u-dye-la-nee
glass	sklenice	sklen-yitse
bottle	láhev	lah-hev
knife	nůž	noozh
fork	vidlička	vid-lich-ka
spoon	lžíce	lzhee-tse

Menu Decoder

biftek	bif-tek	steak
bílé víno	bee-leh vee-no	white wine
bramborové knedlíky	bram-bo-ro-veh kne-dleeki	potato dumplings
brambory	bram-bo-ri	potatoes
chléb	khlehb	bread
cukr	tsukr	sugar
čaj	chay	tea
červené víno	cher-ven-eh vee-no	red wine
grilované	gril-ov-a-neh	grilled
houskové knedlíky	ho-sko-veh kne-dleeki	bread dumplings
hovězí	hov-ye-zee	beef
hranolky	hra-nol-ki	chips
husa	hu-sa	goose
jablko	ya-bl-ko	apple
jehněčí	ye-hnye-chee	lamb
kachna	kakh-na	duck
kapr	ka-pr	carp
káva	kah-va	coffee
kuře	ku-rzhe	chicken
kyselé zelí	kis-el-eh zel-ee	sauerkraut
maso	ma-so	meat
máslo	mah-slo	butter

mléko	mleh-ko	milk
mořská jídla	morzh-skah yeed-la	seafood
párek	paa-rek	sausage
pečený	petsh-en-eh	baked
pečené	pech-en-eh	roast
polévka	po-lehv-ka	soup
pivo	pi-vo	beer
ryba	ri-ba	fish
rýže	ree-zhe	rice
salát	sa-laat/sa-laht	salad
stůl	sool	salt
sýr	seer	cheese
šunka	shun-ka	ham
vařená/ uzená	va-rzhe-nah/ u-zenah	cooked smoked
telecí	te-le-tsee	veal
vajíčko	va-yeech-ko	egg
vařené	va-rzhe-neh	boiled
vepřové	vep-rzho-veh	pork
voda	vo-da	water
zelenina	ze-le-nyi-na	vegetables

Numbers

1	jedna	yed-na
2	dvě	dvye
3	tři	trzhi
4	čtyři	chti-rzhi
5	pět	pyet
6	šest	shest
7	sedm	sedm
8	osm	osm
9	devět	dev-yet
10	deset	de-set
11	jedenáct	ye-de-nahtst
12	dvanáct	dva-nahtst
13	třináct	trzhi-nahtst
14	čtrnáct	chtr-nahtst
15	patnáct	pat-nahtst
16	šestnáct	shest-nahtst
17	sedmnáct	sedm-nahtst
18	osmnáct	osm-nahtst
19	devatenáct	de-va-te-nahtst
20	dvacet	dva-tset
21	dvacet jedna	dva-tset yed-na
22	dvacet dva	dva-tset dva
30	třicet	trzhi-tset
40	čtyřicet	chti-rzhi-tset
50	padesát	pa-de-saht
60	šedesát	she-de-saht
70	sedmdesát	sedm-de-saht
80	osmdesát	osm-de-saht
90	devadesát	de-va-de-saht
100	sto	sto
1,000	tisíc	tyi-seets
2,000	dva tisíce	dva tyi-see-tse
5,000	pět tisíc	pyet tyi-seets
1,000,000	milión	mi-li-ohn

Time

one minute	jedna minuta	yed-na mi-nu-ta
one hour	jedna hodina	yed-na ho-dyi-na
half an hour	půl hodiny	pool ho-dyi-ni
day	den	den
week	týden	tee-den
Monday	pondělí	pon-dye-lee
Tuesday	úterý	oo-te-ree
Wednesday	středa	strzhe-da
Thursday	čtvrtek	chtvr-tek
Friday	pátek	pah-tek
Saturday	sobota	so-bo-ta
Sunday	neděle	ned-yel-e

ACKNOWLEDGMENTS

This edition updated by

Contributors Mark Baker, Joesph Reaney

Senior Editor Alison McGill

Project Editor Charlie Baker

Senior Designers Laura O'Brien, Stuti Tiwari

Art Editor Bandana Paul

Editor Vineet Singh

Proofreader Ben Ffrancon Dowds

Indexer Helen Peters

Picture Research Manager Taiyaba Khatoon

Senior Picture Researcher Nishwan Rasool

Picture Research Team Priya Singh, Manpreet Kaur, Samrajkumar.S

Publishing Assistant Simona Velikova

Jacket Designer Laura O'Brien

Senior Cartographer Subhashree Bharati

Senior Cartographic Editor James Macdonald

Cartography Manager Suresh Kumar

Senior DTP Designer Tanveer Zaidi

DTP Designer Rohit Rojal

Senior Production Manager Balwant Singh

Image Retouching-Production Manager Pankaj Sharma

Production Controller Kariss Ainsworth

Managing Editors Beverly Smart, Hollie Teague

Managing Art Editor Gemma Doyle

Senior Managing Art Editor Priyanka Thakur

Art Director Maxine Pedliham

Publishing Director Georgina Dee

DK would like to thank the following for their contribution to the previous editions: Hilary Bird, Demetrio Carrasco, John Coletti, Paul Franklin, Kathryn Glendenning, Nancy Mikula, Rough Guides/Angus Osborn, Rough Guides/ Susannah Sayler, Jonathan Schultz, Tony Souter, Linda Whitwam.

The publisher would like to thank the following for their kind permission to reproduce their photographs:

(Key: a-above; b-below/bottom; c-centre; f-far; l-left; r-right; t-top)

Alamy Stock Photo: Andrey Akimov 66b, Album 54, Belikart 63tr, Carlo Bollo 9br, Petr Bonek 8, Ian Bottle 59b, Peter Forsberg / CR 47b, © Zdenek Pridal / CTK Photo 93b, CTK 10bl, 56b, CTK Photo / Katerina Sulova 12cr, Katerina Sulova / CTK Photo 93t, Ian Dagnall 89t, Britta Pedersen / dpa 11, dpa picture alliance 57, Robert Dziewulski 23bl, Adam Eastland 13bl, eFesenko, 26cla, GL Archive 9tl, Manfred Glueck 72, Shim Harno 56t, Rieger Bertrand / Hemis.fr 15tl, Historic Images 41cla, Home Bird 77b, imageBROKER / Moritz Wolf 98, imageBROKER. com GmbH & Co. KG / Walter G. Allgöwer 33cla, Images&Stories 21cla, INTERFOTO / History 61, Ivoha 52t, kaprik 127t, Brenda Kean 105t, John Kellerman 68t, Vitalii Kliuiev 13cl, Art Kowalsky 44-45b, Loop Images Ltd / Anna Stowe 83t, MB_ Photo 114-115t, Hercules Milas 24, MiraMira 101, Jim Monk 106t, John Norman 38b, Cum Okolo 12br, 13cl (8), 15br, 40b, 60t, 73, 74t, 92, 95, 103, 121b, PBarchive 25, 39, J. Pie 111br, 124t, PjrStatues 111bl, PjrTravel 10clb, 59t, 90t, Peter Forsberg / Praha 128, Prisma Archivo 9cr, Mieneke Andeweg-van Rijn 62-63, Shawshots 10cla, Charles Stirling (Travel) 71, stockex 13cla, Lana Sundman 31, Liba Taylor 84, Maksym Tsalko 30, Steve Tulley 13clb, Lucas Vallecillos 75t, volkerpreusser 124b, Mike Withers 64b, Yegorovnick 67t, Zoonar / Kai Michael Neuhold 53t.

Aromi: 133.

Artel Glass: 81t.

Bakeshop Praha: 116.

Depositphotos Inc: VividaPhoto 113t.

Dorling Kindersley: Jiri Kopriva 122, Vladimir Kozlik 58b, Frantisek Preucil 114b, Stanislav Tereba 82.

Dreamstime.com: Anton Aleksenko 14, 52b, Sorin Colac 34br, Dziewul 26b, Anton Eine 76t, Evgeniy Fesenko 34-35t, 37b, Veronika Galkina 16crb, Marian Garai 131, Diego Grandi 23br, 65, Grounder 106-107b, Natalia Hanin 44cla, Nataliya Hora 97t, Josefkubes 33tc, Kaprik 66t, Zoran Kompar 21bc, Madeleinesteinbach 81b, Kirill Makarov 51t, Marietf 20cla, Andres Garcia Martin 90b, Roman Milert 37t, Mistervlad 28b, Martin Molcan 12cra, Montypeter 85, Luciano Mortula 21cr, Marketa Novakova 130, Positivetravelart 74-75b, Nikita Pritykin 70, Pytyczech 6-7, 17, 99tl, Dietmar Rauscher 78t, Pavel Rezac 87, Rumata7 97b, Vladimir Sazonov 120, Jozef Sedmak 63cra, Josef Skacel 129b, Stevanovicigor 9tr, 50b, Stockfotocz 76b, Jana Telenská 77t, Thecriss 119b, Anibal Trejo 23crb, Uko_jesita 33tr, Wrangel 80b, Yakub88 27t.

A NOTE FROM DK

The rate at which the world is changing is constantly keeping the DK travel team on our toes. While we've worked hard to ensure that this edition of Prague is accurate and up-to-date, we know that opening hours alter, standards shift, prices fluctuate, places close and new ones pop up in their stead. So, if you notice we've got something wrong or left something out, we want to hear about it. Please get in touch at travelguides@dk.com

Within each Top 10 list in this book, no hierarchy of quality or popularity is implied. All 10 are, in the editor's opinion, of roughly equal merit.

Penguin
Random
House

First edition 2003

Published in Great Britain by Dorling Kindersley Limited,
DK, One Embassy Gardens, 8 Viaduct Gardens,
London SW11 7BW, UK

The authorised representative in the EEA is
Dorling Kindersley Verlag GmbH. Arnulfstr.
124, 80636 Munich, Germany

Published in the United States by DK Publishing,
1745 Broadway, 20th Floor, New York, NY 10019, USA

A CIP catalog record for this book
is available from the British Library.

A catalog record for this book is available
from the Library of Congress.

ISSN: 1479-344X
ISBN: 978-0-2416-7671-4

Printed and bound in China

www.dk.com

MIX
Paper | Supporting
responsible forestry
FSC™ C018179